STAR WARS

THE CLONE WARS

IN SERVICE OF THE REPUBLIC

D1125200

DESIGNER **DAVID NESTELLE**

ASSISTANT EDITOR **FREDDYE LINS**

EDITOR **RANDY STRADLEY**

PUBLISHER **MIKE RICHARDSON**

Special thanks to Jann Moorhead, David Anderman, Troy Alders, Leland Chee, Sue Rostoni, and Carol Roeder at Lucas Licensing.

Published by Dark Horse Books, a division of Dark Horse Comics, Inc.
10956 SE Main Street, Milwaukie, OR 97222

darkhorse.com | starwars.com

To find a comics shop in your area, call the Comic Shop Locator Service toll-free at **1.888.266.4226**
First edition: June 2010 | ISBN 978-1-59582-487-5

Library of Congress Cataloging-in-Publication Data

Star Wars, the clone wars : in service of the republic.
    p. cm.
"This volume collects issues #7-#9 of the Dark Horse comic-book series Star Wars: The Clone Wars, and Star Wars: The Clone Wars-Gauntlet of Death from Free Comic Book Day 2009."
ISBN 978-1-59582-487-5
1. Graphic novels. I. Gilroy, Henry. II. Melching, Steven. III. Star Wars, the clone wars (Television program) IV. Title: Clone Wars.
PN6728.S73S75 2010
741.5'973–dc22

                        2010000194

10 9 8 7 6 5 4 3 2 1
Printed at Midas Printing International, Ltd., Huizhou, China

STAR WARS: THE CLONE WARS—IN SERVICE OF THE REPUBLIC

This volume collects issues #7–#9 of the Dark Horse comic-book series *Star Wars: The Clone Wars*, and *Star Wars: The Clone Wars—Gauntlet of Death* from Free Comic Book Day 2009.

STAR WARS

THE CLONE WARS

IN SERVICE OF THE REPUBLIC

IN SERVICE OF THE REPUBLIC

SCRIPT **HENRY GILROY**
STEVEN MELCHING

PENCILS **SCOTT HEPBURN**

INKS **DAN PARSONS**

COLORS **MICHAEL E. WIGGAM**

GAUNTLET OF DEATH

SCRIPT **HENRY GILROY**

ART **RAMÓN K. PÉREZ**

LETTERING **MICHAEL HEISLER**

COVER ART **RAMÓN K. PÉREZ**

DARK HORSE BOOKS®

THE RISE OF THE EMPIRE
1000–0 YEARS BEFORE *STAR WARS: A NEW HOPE*

The events in these stories take place approximately
twenty-two years before the Battle of Yavin.

After the seeming final defeat of the Sith, the Republic enters a state
of complacency. In the waning years of the Republic, the Senate is rife
with corruption, and the ambitious Senator Palpatine has himself elected
Supreme Chancellor. This is the era of the prequel trilogy.

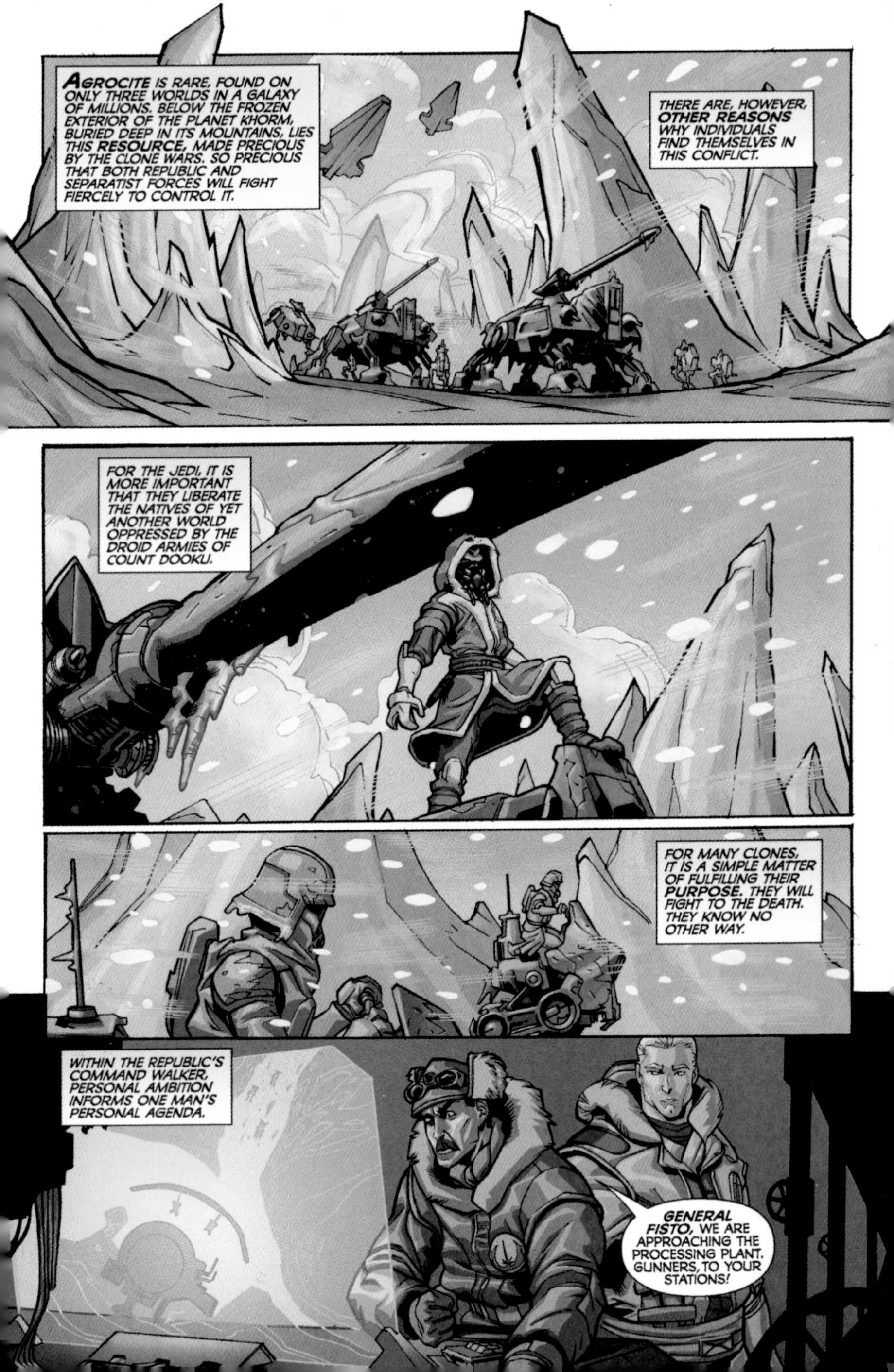
AGROCITE IS RARE, FOUND ON ONLY THREE WORLDS IN A GALAXY OF MILLIONS. BELOW THE FROZEN EXTERIOR OF THE PLANET KHORM, BURIED DEEP IN ITS MOUNTAINS, LIES THIS RESOURCE, MADE PRECIOUS BY THE CLONE WARS. SO PRECIOUS THAT BOTH REPUBLIC AND SEPARATIST FORCES WILL FIGHT FIERCELY TO CONTROL IT.
THERE ARE, HOWEVER, OTHER REASONS WHY INDIVIDUALS FIND THEMSELVES IN THIS CONFLICT.
FOR THE JEDI, IT IS MORE IMPORTANT THAT THEY LIBERATE THE NATIVES OF YET ANOTHER WORLD OPPRESSED BY THE DROID ARMIES OF COUNT DOOKU.
FOR MANY CLONES, IT IS A SIMPLE MATTER OF FULFILLING THEIR PURPOSE. THEY WILL FIGHT TO THE DEATH. THEY KNOW NO OTHER WAY.
WITHIN THE REPUBLIC'S COMMAND WALKER, PERSONAL AMBITION INFORMS ONE MAN'S PERSONAL AGENDA.
GENERAL FISTO, WE ARE APPROACHING THE PROCESSING PLANT. GUNNERS, TO YOUR STATIONS!

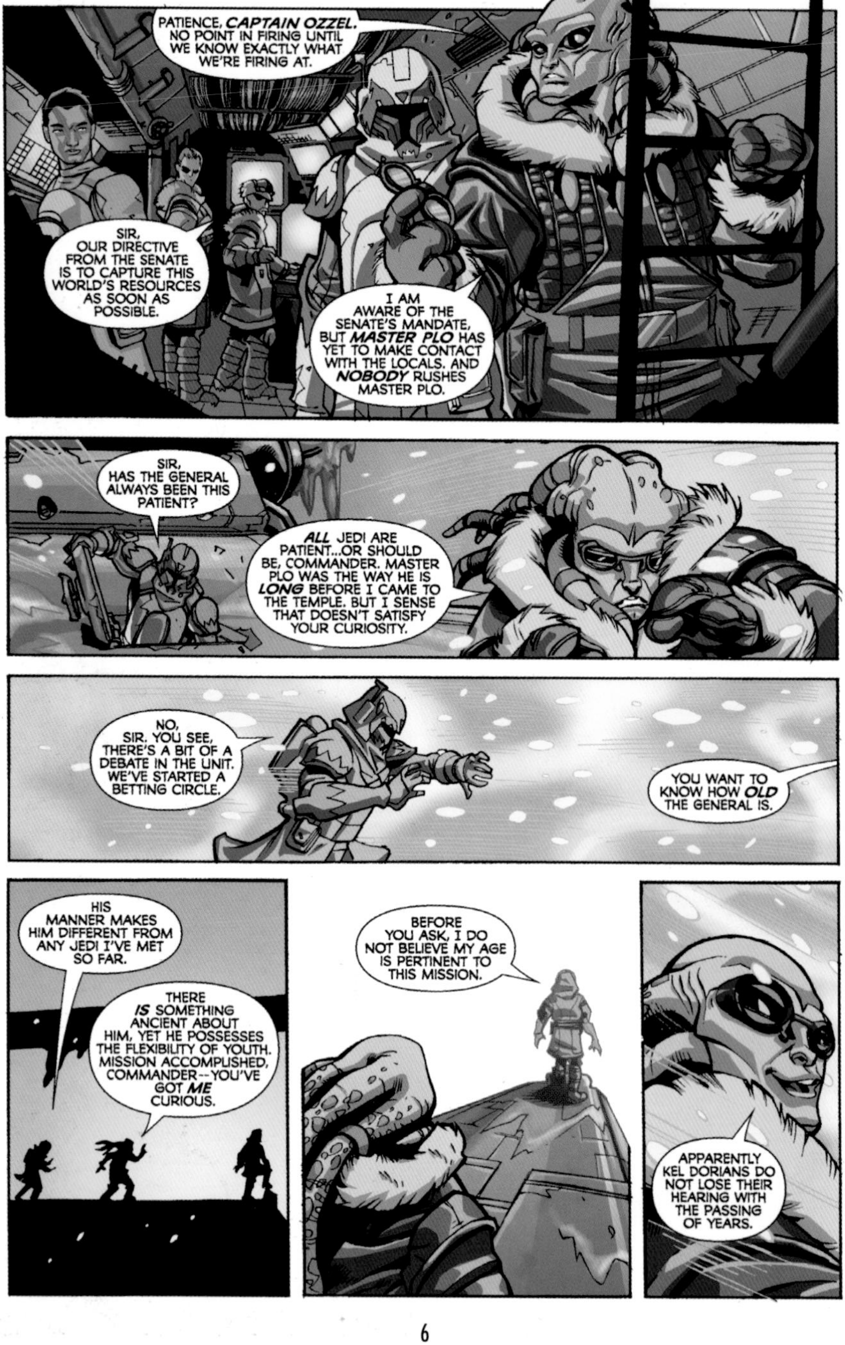

PATIENCE, CAPTAIN OZZEL. NO POINT IN FIRING UNTIL WE KNOW EXACTLY WHAT WE'RE FIRING AT.
SIR, OUR DIRECTIVE FROM THE SENATE IS TO CAPTURE THIS WORLD'S RESOURCES AS SOON AS POSSIBLE.
I AM AWARE OF THE SENATE'S MANDATE, BUT MASTER PLO HAS YET TO MAKE CONTACT WITH THE LOCALS. AND NOBODY RUSHES MASTER PLO.
SIR, HAS THE GENERAL ALWAYS BEEN THIS PATIENT?
ALL JEDI ARE PATIENT...OR SHOULD BE, COMMANDER. MASTER PLO WAS THE WAY HE IS LONG BEFORE I CAME TO THE TEMPLE. BUT I SENSE THAT DOESN'T SATISFY YOUR CURIOSITY.
NO, SIR. YOU SEE, THERE'S A BIT OF A DEBATE IN THE UNIT. WE'VE STARTED A BETTING CIRCLE.
YOU WANT TO KNOW HOW OLD THE GENERAL IS.
HIS MANNER MAKES HIM DIFFERENT FROM ANY JEDI I'VE MET SO FAR.
THERE IS SOMETHING ANCIENT ABOUT HIM, YET HE POSSESSES THE FLEXIBILITY OF YOUTH. MISSION ACCOMPLISHED, COMMANDER--YOU'VE GOT ME CURIOUS.
BEFORE YOU ASK, I DO NOT BELIEVE MY AGE IS PERTINENT TO THIS MISSION.
APPARENTLY KEL DORIANS DO NOT LOSE THEIR HEARING WITH THE PASSING OF YEARS.

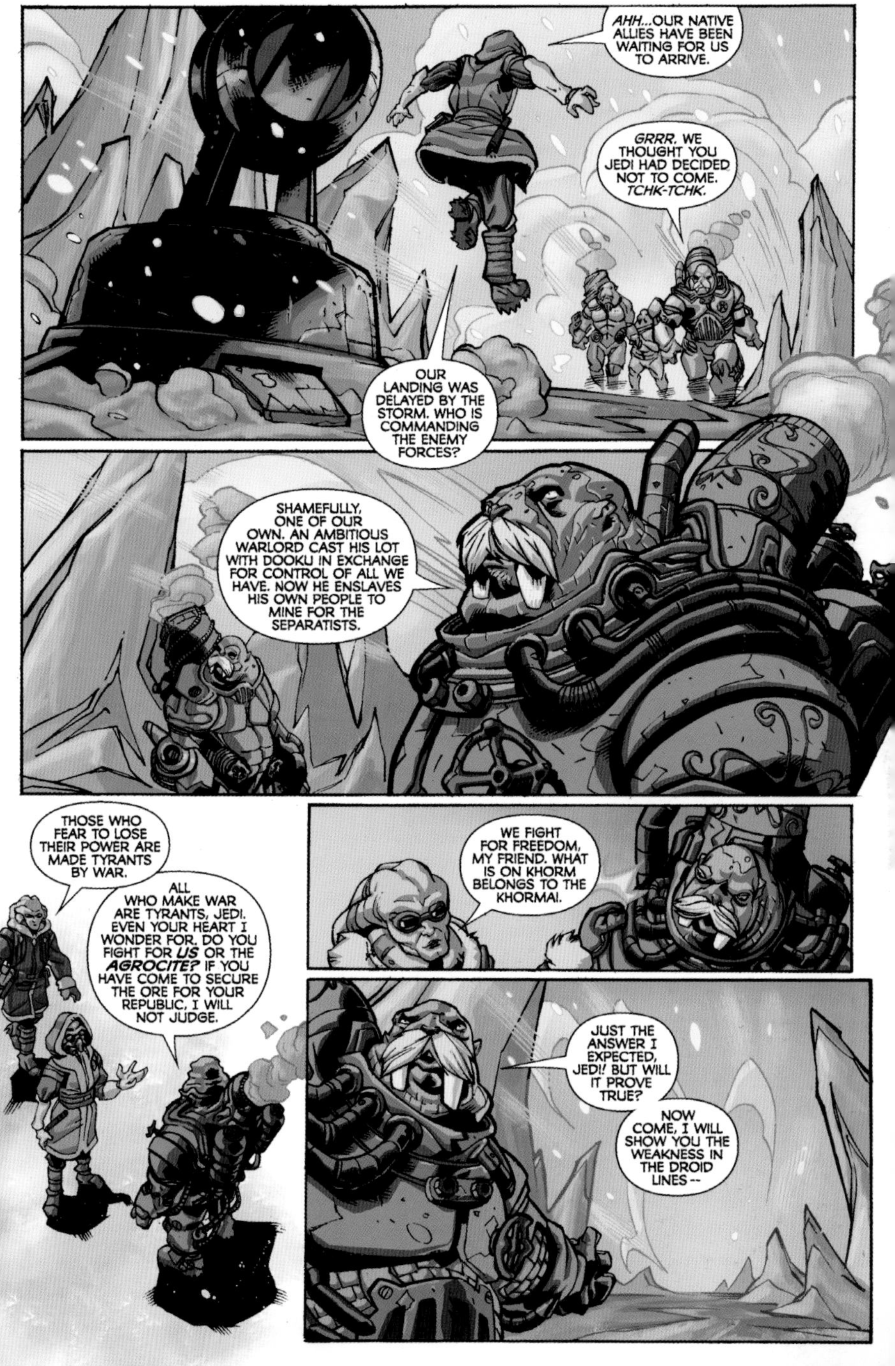
AHH...OUR NATIVE ALLIES HAVE BEEN WAITING FOR US TO ARRIVE.
GRRR. WE THOUGHT YOU JEDI HAD DECIDED NOT TO COME. TCHK-TCHK.
OUR LANDING WAS DELAYED BY THE STORM. WHO IS COMMANDING THE ENEMY FORCES?
SHAMEFULLY, ONE OF OUR OWN. AN AMBITIOUS WARLORD CAST HIS LOT WITH DOOKU IN EXCHANGE FOR CONTROL OF ALL WE HAVE. NOW HE ENSLAVES HIS OWN PEOPLE TO MINE FOR THE SEPARATISTS.
THOSE WHO FEAR TO LOSE THEIR POWER ARE MADE TYRANTS BY WAR.
ALL WHO MAKE WAR ARE TYRANTS, JEDI. EVEN YOUR HEART I WONDER FOR. DO YOU FIGHT FOR US OR THE AGROCITE? IF YOU HAVE COME TO SECURE THE ORE FOR YOUR REPUBLIC, I WILL NOT JUDGE.
WE FIGHT FOR FREEDOM, MY FRIEND. WHAT IS ON KHORM BELONGS TO THE KHORMAI.
JUST THE ANSWER I EXPECTED, JEDI! BUT WILL IT PROVE TRUE?
NOW COME, I WILL SHOW YOU THE WEAKNESS IN THE DROID LINES --

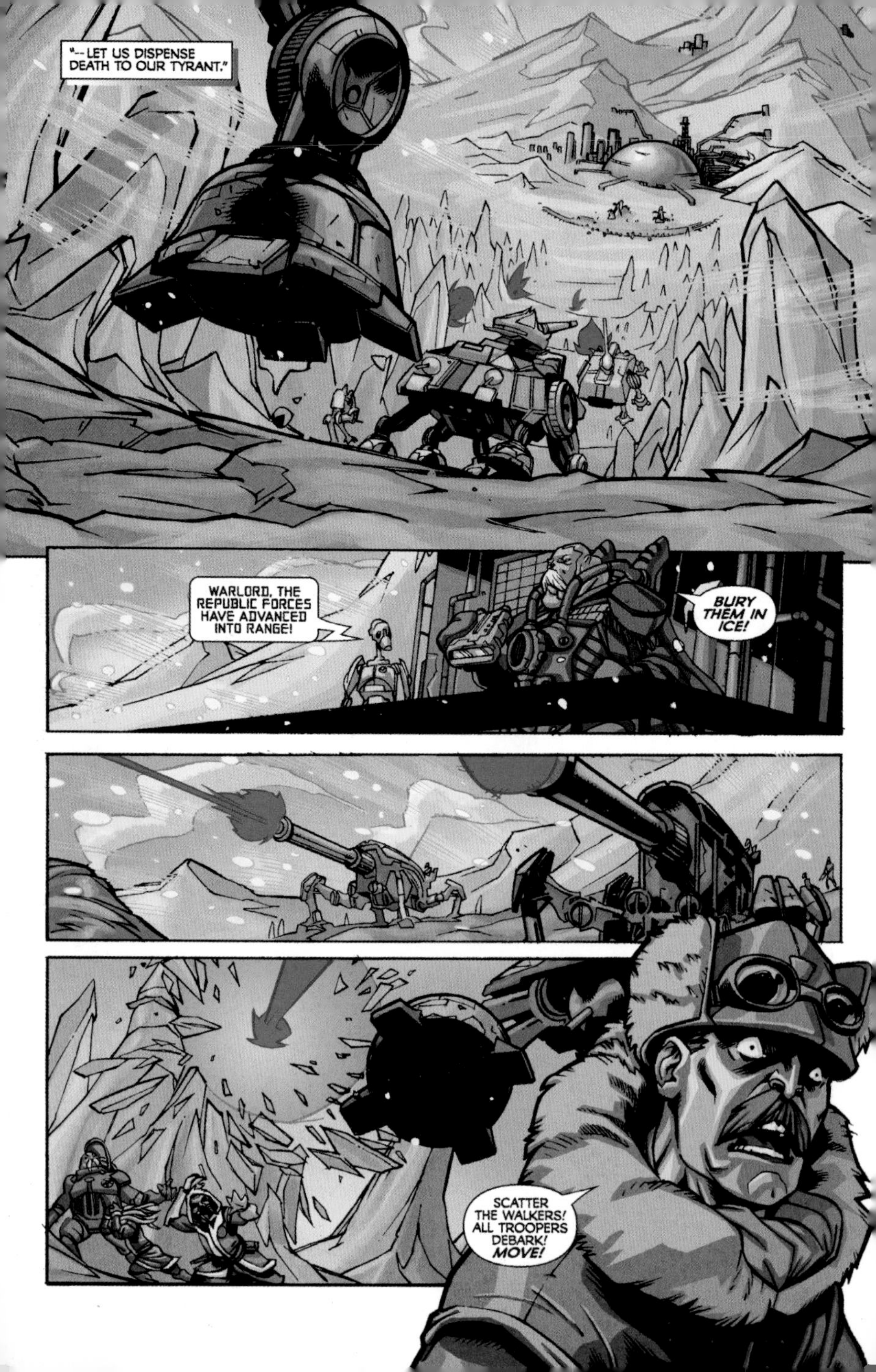
"--LET US DISPENSE DEATH TO OUR TYRANT."
WARLORD, THE REPUBLIC FORCES HAVE ADVANCED INTO RANGE!
BURY THEM IN ICE!
SCATTER THE WALKERS! ALL TROOPERS DEBARK! MOVE!

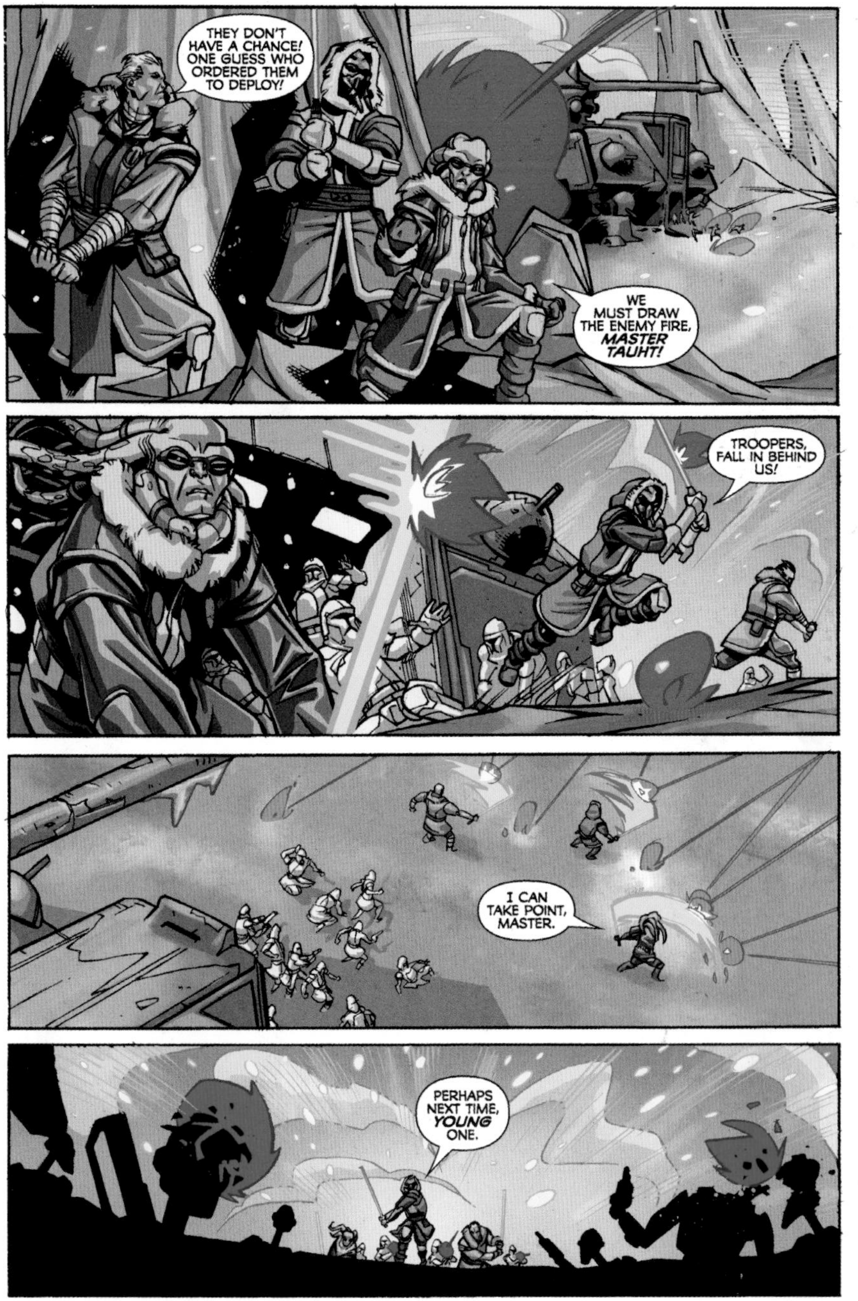
THEY DON'T HAVE A CHANCE! ONE GUESS WHO ORDERED THEM TO DEPLOY!
WE MUST DRAW THE ENEMY FIRE, *MASTER TAUHT!*
TROOPERS, FALL IN BEHIND US!
I CAN TAKE POINT, MASTER.
PERHAPS NEXT TIME, *YOUNG* ONE.

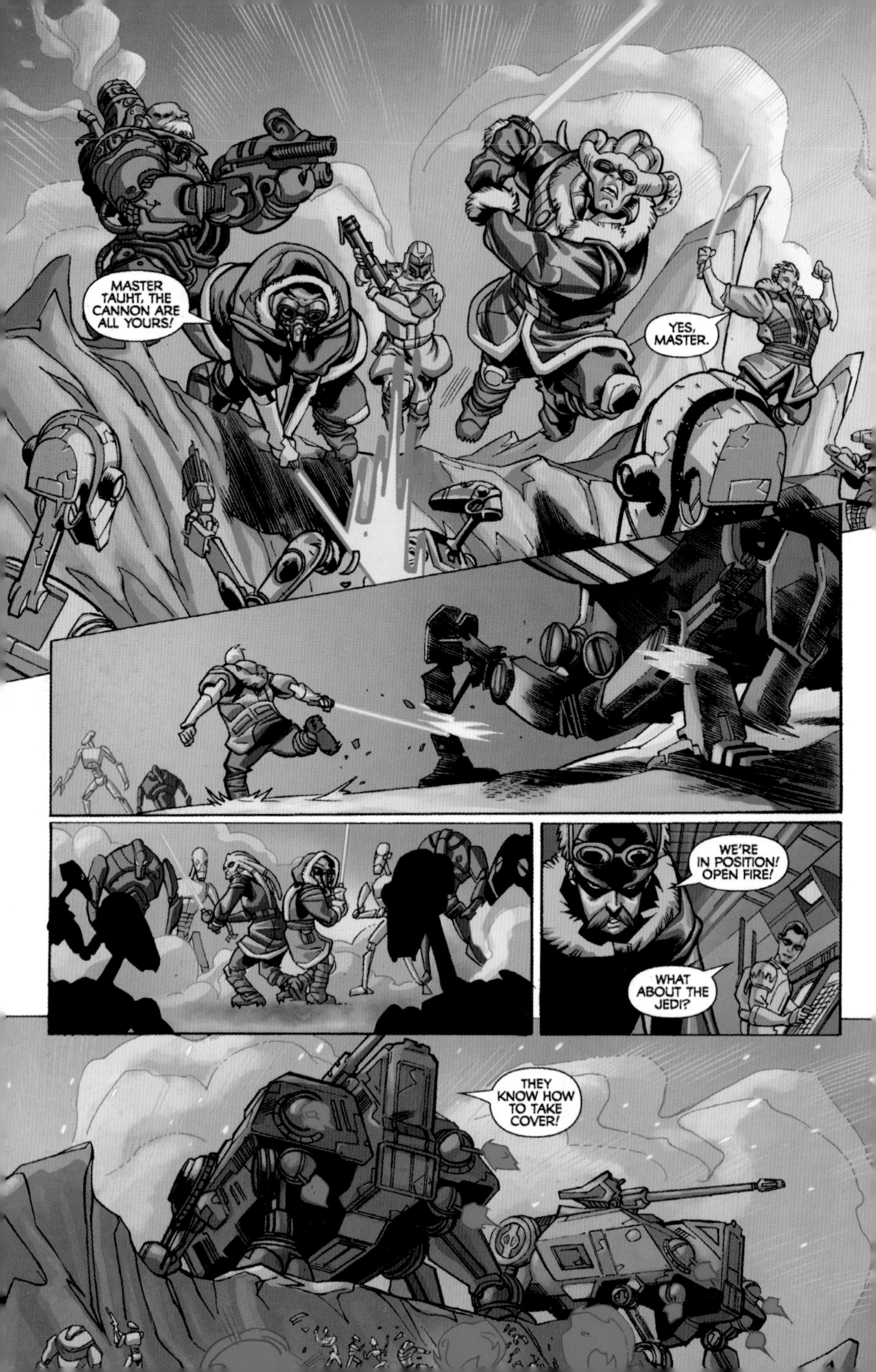
MASTER TAUHT, THE CANNON ARE ALL YOURS!
YES, MASTER.
WE'RE IN POSITION! OPEN FIRE!
WHAT ABOUT THE JEDI?
THEY KNOW HOW TO TAKE COVER!

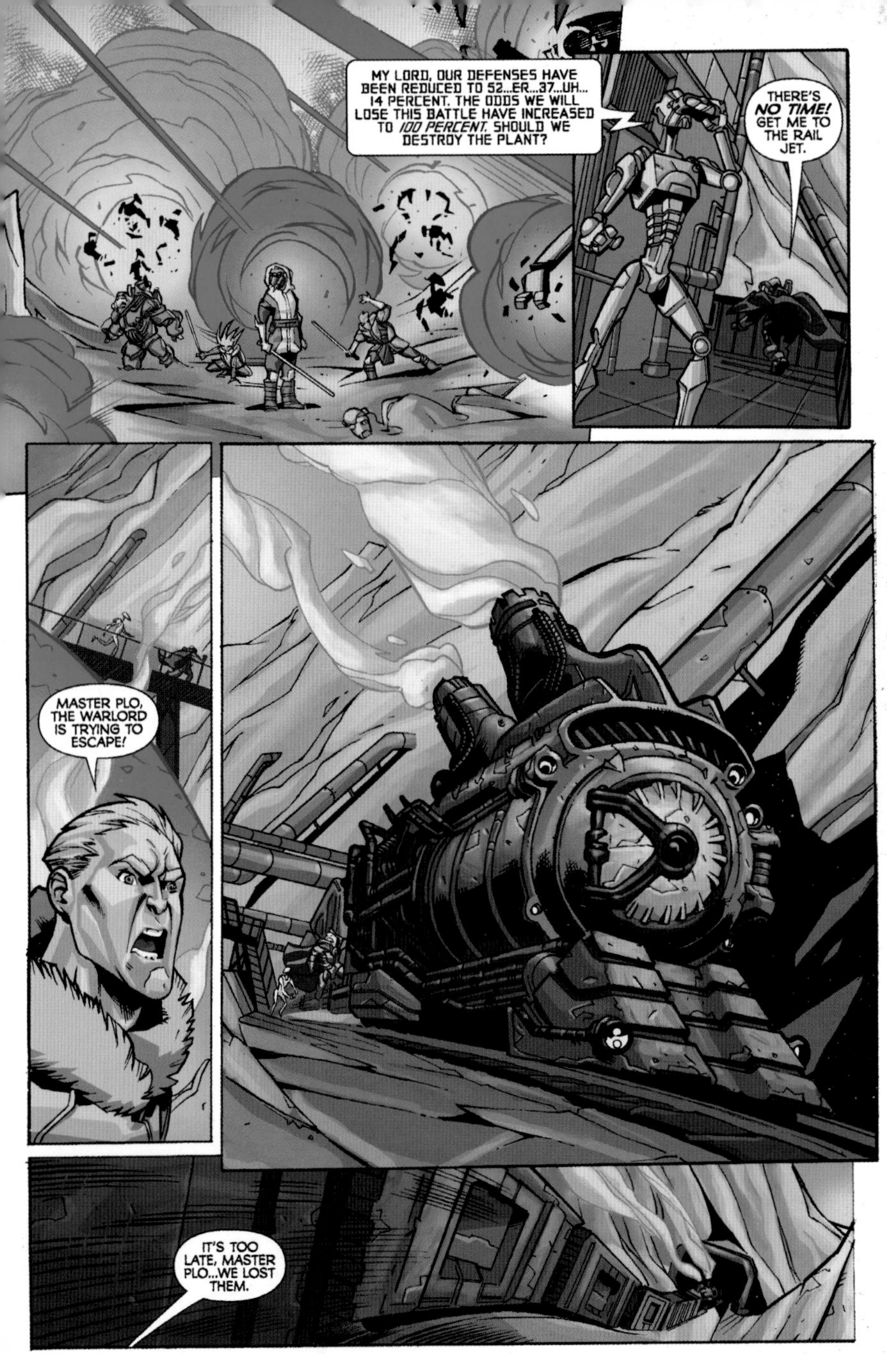
MY LORD, OUR DEFENSES HAVE BEEN REDUCED TO 52...ER...37...UH... 14 PERCENT. THE ODDS WE WILL LOSE THIS BATTLE HAVE INCREASED TO *100 PERCENT.* SHOULD WE DESTROY THE PLANT?
THERE'S ***NO TIME!*** GET ME TO THE RAIL JET.
MASTER PLO, THE WARLORD IS TRYING TO ESCAPE!
IT'S TOO LATE, MASTER PLO...WE LOST THEM.

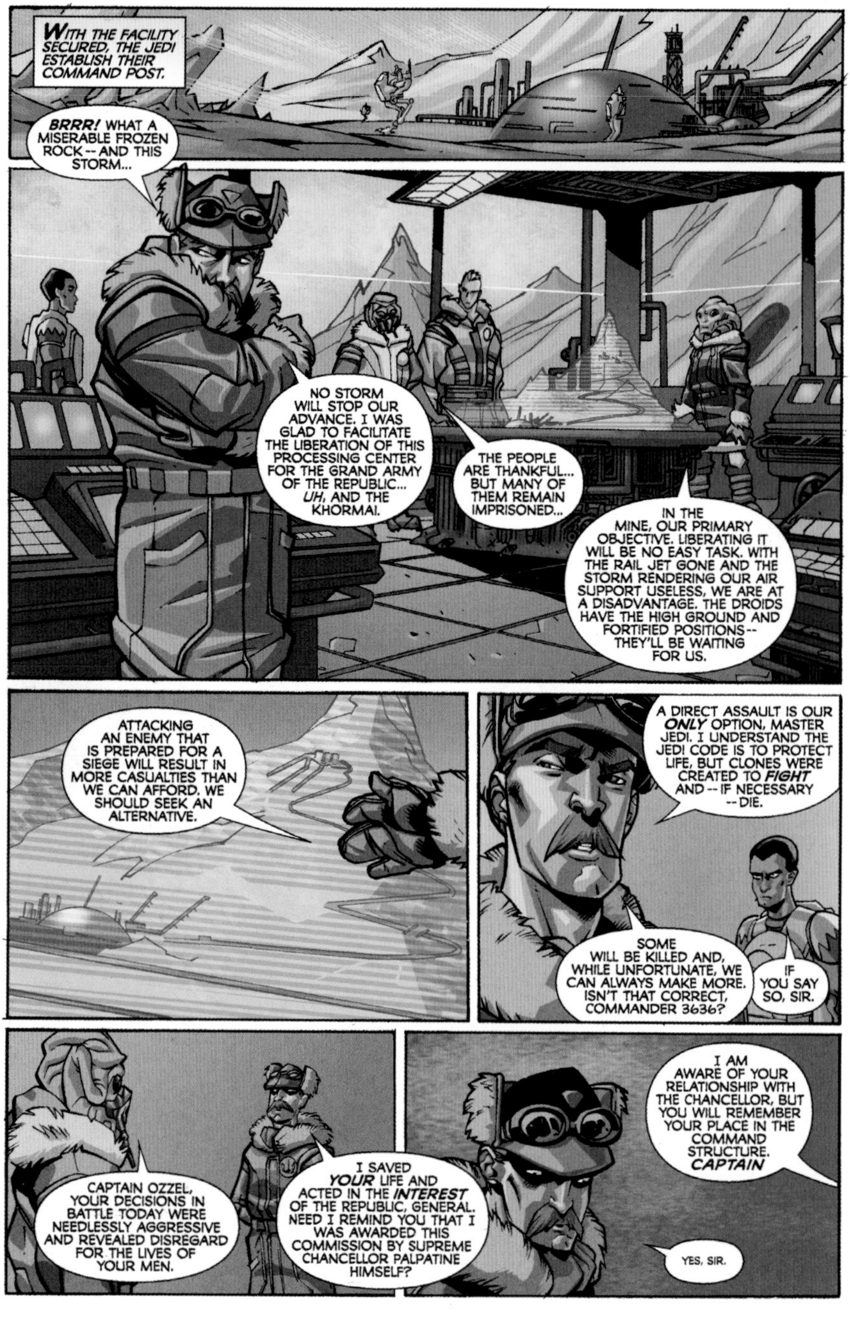
WITH THE FACILITY SECURED, THE JEDI ESTABLISH THEIR COMMAND POST.
BRRR! WHAT A MISERABLE FROZEN ROCK -- AND THIS STORM...
NO STORM WILL STOP OUR ADVANCE. I WAS GLAD TO FACILITATE THE LIBERATION OF THIS PROCESSING CENTER FOR THE GRAND ARMY OF THE REPUBLIC... UH, AND THE KHORMAI.
THE PEOPLE ARE THANKFUL... BUT MANY OF THEM REMAIN IMPRISONED...
IN THE MINE, OUR PRIMARY OBJECTIVE. LIBERATING IT WILL BE NO EASY TASK. WITH THE RAIL JET GONE AND THE STORM RENDERING OUR AIR SUPPORT USELESS, WE ARE AT A DISADVANTAGE. THE DROIDS HAVE THE HIGH GROUND AND FORTIFIED POSITIONS -- THEY'LL BE WAITING FOR US.
ATTACKING AN ENEMY THAT IS PREPARED FOR A SIEGE WILL RESULT IN MORE CASUALTIES THAN WE CAN AFFORD. WE SHOULD SEEK AN ALTERNATIVE.
A DIRECT ASSAULT IS OUR ONLY OPTION, MASTER JEDI. I UNDERSTAND THE JEDI CODE IS TO PROTECT LIFE, BUT CLONES WERE CREATED TO FIGHT AND -- IF NECESSARY -- DIE.
SOME WILL BE KILLED AND, WHILE UNFORTUNATE, WE CAN ALWAYS MAKE MORE. ISN'T THAT CORRECT, COMMANDER 3636?
IF YOU SAY SO, SIR.
CAPTAIN OZZEL, YOUR DECISIONS IN BATTLE TODAY WERE NEEDLESSLY AGGRESSIVE AND REVEALED DISREGARD FOR THE LIVES OF YOUR MEN.
I SAVED YOUR LIFE AND ACTED IN THE INTEREST OF THE REPUBLIC, GENERAL. NEED I REMIND YOU THAT I WAS AWARDED THIS COMMISSION BY SUPREME CHANCELLOR PALPATINE HIMSELF?
I AM AWARE OF YOUR RELATIONSHIP WITH THE CHANCELLOR, BUT YOU WILL REMEMBER YOUR PLACE IN THE COMMAND STRUCTURE. CAPTAIN
YES, SIR.

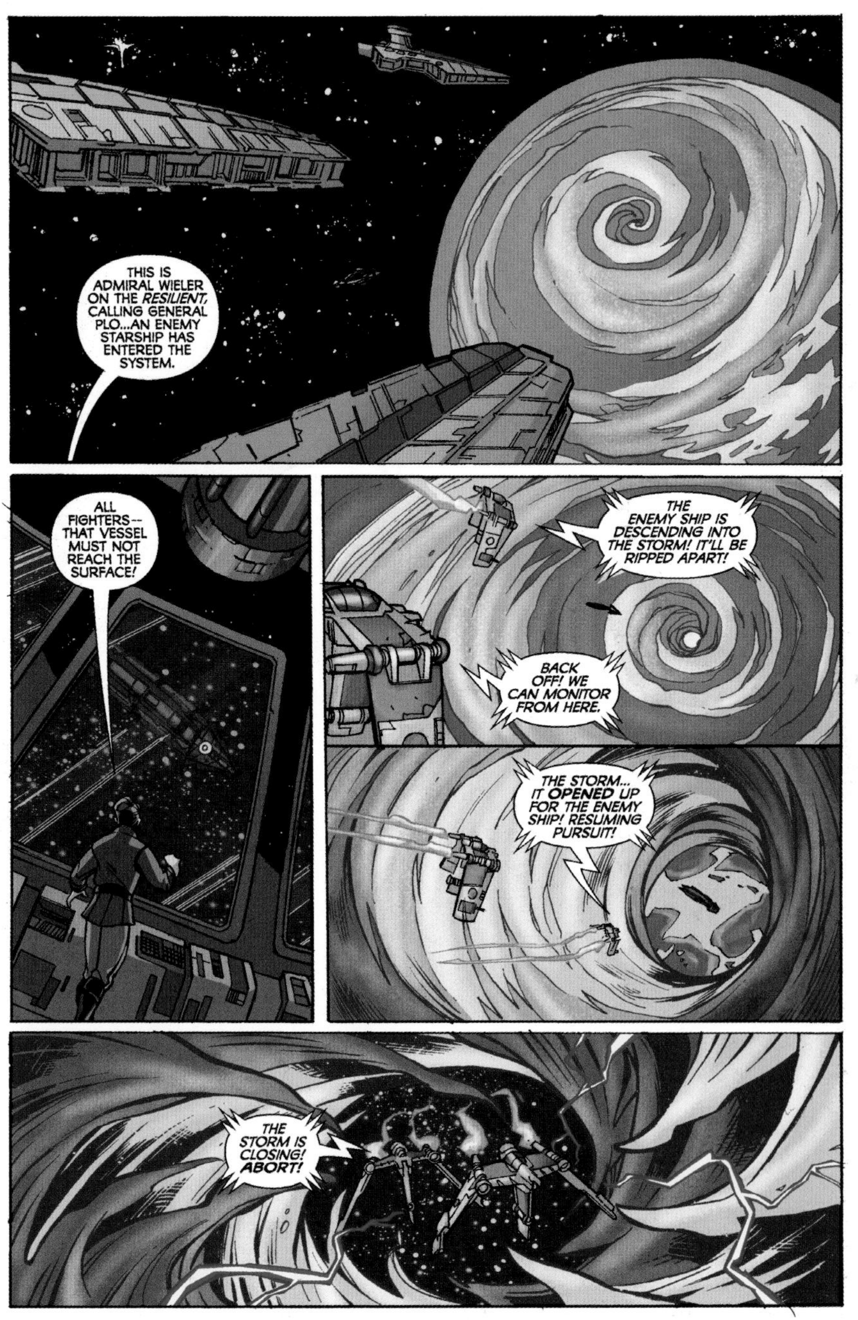
THIS IS ADMIRAL WIELER ON THE *RESILIENT,* CALLING GENERAL PLO...AN ENEMY STARSHIP HAS ENTERED THE SYSTEM.
ALL FIGHTERS-- THAT VESSEL MUST NOT REACH THE SURFACE!
THE ENEMY SHIP IS DESCENDING INTO THE STORM! IT'LL BE RIPPED APART!
BACK OFF! WE CAN MONITOR FROM HERE.
THE STORM... IT **OPENED** UP FOR THE ENEMY SHIP! RESUMING PURSUIT!
THE STORM IS CLOSING! **ABORT!**

THE ENEMY GOT THROUGH AND...THE STORM RE-FORMED TO FULL STRENGTH. OUR FIGHTERS WERE LOST.

THE ATMOSPHERIC DISTORTION IS CENTERED NEAR YOUR PRIMARY OBJECTIVE.

WHICH MEANS THE ENEMY MUST HAVE SOME SORT OF CLIMATE-CONTROL STATION NEAR THEIR BASE. CLONE INTELLIGENCE HAS REPORTED THE SEPARATISTS' ATTEMPTS TO ACQUIRE THE TECHNOLOGY.

AND SO THEY HAVE. IF WE CAN FIND...AND ELIMINATE THAT STATION, WE CAN UTILIZE OUR AIR SUPPORT TO LIBERATE THE MINE--

-- AND FREE THE INHABITANTS BEING HELD THERE.

YOU DON'T EXPECT ME TO GO ON SOME WILD SEEK-AND-DESTROY MISSION?

NO, CAPTAIN. MASTER FISTO AND MYSELF WILL LEAD THE MISSION.

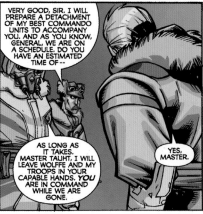

VERY GOOD, SIR. I WILL PREPARE A DETACHMENT OF MY BEST COMMANDO UNITS TO ACCOMPANY YOU. AND AS YOU KNOW, GENERAL, WE ARE ON A SCHEDULE. DO YOU HAVE AN ESTIMATED TIME OF --

AS LONG AS IT TAKES, MASTER TAUHT. I WILL LEAVE WOLFFE AND MY TROOPS IN YOUR CAPABLE HANDS. *YOU* ARE IN COMMAND WHILE WE ARE GONE.

YES, MASTER.

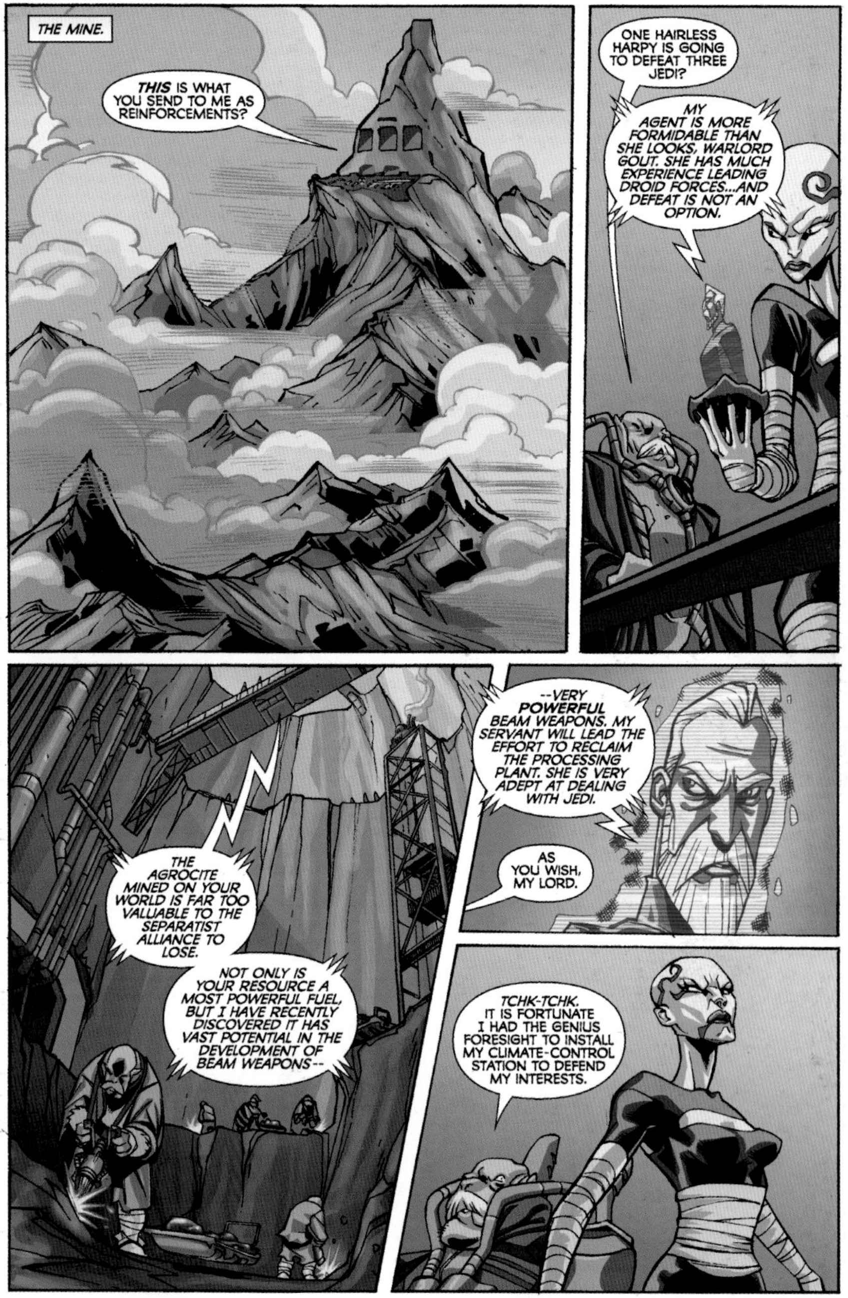
THE MINE.
THIS IS WHAT YOU SEND TO ME AS REINFORCEMENTS?
ONE HAIRLESS HARPY IS GOING TO DEFEAT THREE JEDI?
MY AGENT IS MORE FORMIDABLE THAN SHE LOOKS, WARLORD GOUT. SHE HAS MUCH EXPERIENCE LEADING DROID FORCES...AND DEFEAT IS NOT AN OPTION.
THE AGROCITE MINED ON YOUR WORLD IS FAR TOO VALUABLE TO THE SEPARATIST ALLIANCE TO LOSE.
NOT ONLY IS YOUR RESOURCE A MOST POWERFUL FUEL, BUT I HAVE RECENTLY DISCOVERED IT HAS VAST POTENTIAL IN THE DEVELOPMENT OF BEAM WEAPONS--
--VERY POWERFUL BEAM WEAPONS. MY SERVANT WILL LEAD THE EFFORT TO RECLAIM THE PROCESSING PLANT. SHE IS VERY ADEPT AT DEALING WITH JEDI.
AS YOU WISH, MY LORD.
TCHK-TCHK. IT IS FORTUNATE I HAD THE GENIUS FORESIGHT TO INSTALL MY CLIMATE-CONTROL STATION TO DEFEND MY INTERESTS.

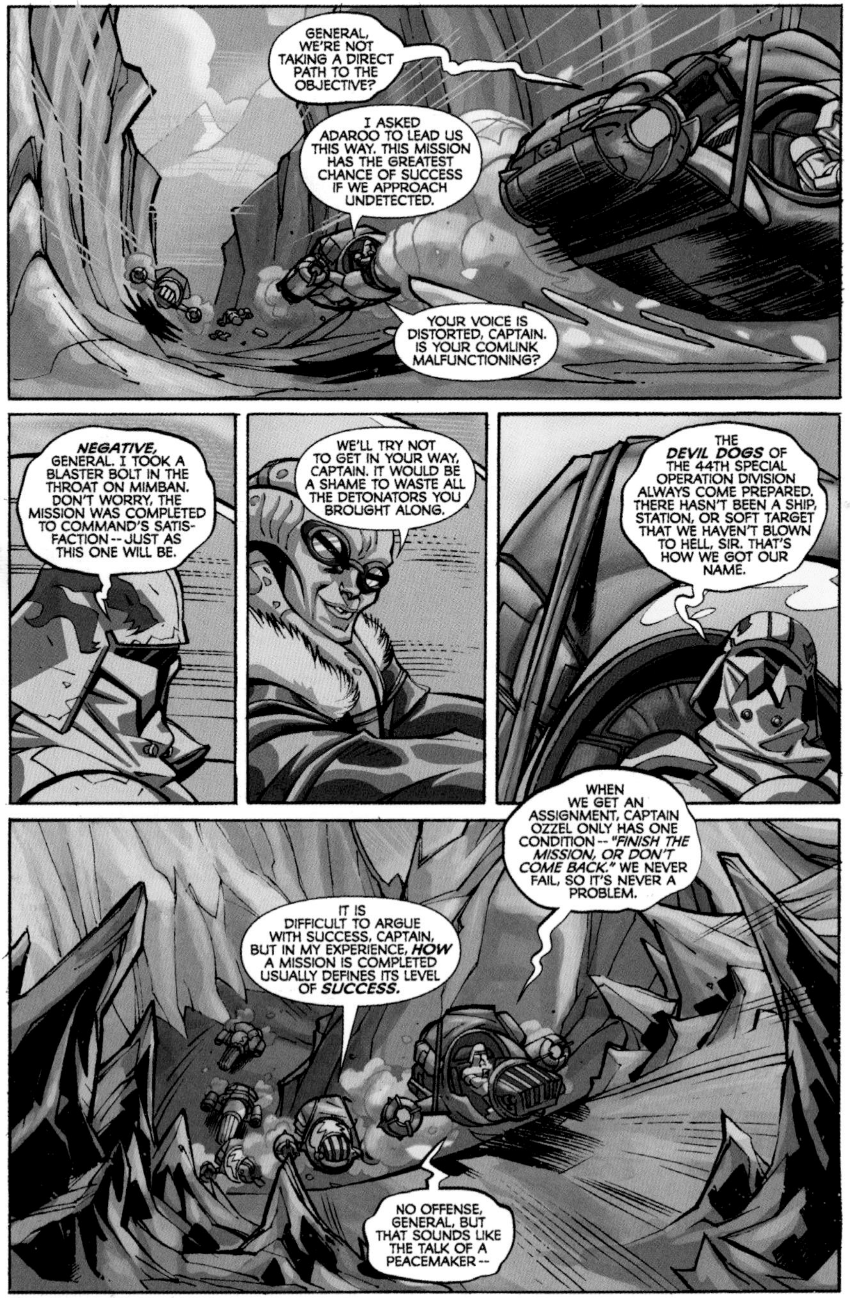
GENERAL, WE'RE NOT TAKING A DIRECT PATH TO THE OBJECTIVE?
I ASKED ADAROO TO LEAD US THIS WAY. THIS MISSION HAS THE GREATEST CHANCE OF SUCCESS IF WE APPROACH UNDETECTED.
YOUR VOICE IS DISTORTED, CAPTAIN. IS YOUR COMLINK MALFUNCTIONING?
NEGATIVE, GENERAL. I TOOK A BLASTER BOLT IN THE THROAT ON MIMBAN. DON'T WORRY, THE MISSION WAS COMPLETED TO COMMAND'S SATIS-FACTION -- JUST AS THIS ONE WILL BE.
WE'LL TRY NOT TO GET IN YOUR WAY, CAPTAIN. IT WOULD BE A SHAME TO WASTE ALL THE DETONATORS YOU BROUGHT ALONG.
THE DEVIL DOGS OF THE 44TH SPECIAL OPERATION DIVISION ALWAYS COME PREPARED. THERE HASN'T BEEN A SHIP, STATION, OR SOFT TARGET THAT WE HAVEN'T BLOWN TO HELL, SIR. THAT'S HOW WE GOT OUR NAME.
WHEN WE GET AN ASSIGNMENT, CAPTAIN OZZEL ONLY HAS ONE CONDITION -- "FINISH THE MISSION, OR DON'T COME BACK." WE NEVER FAIL, SO IT'S NEVER A PROBLEM.
IT IS DIFFICULT TO ARGUE WITH SUCCESS, CAPTAIN, BUT IN MY EXPERIENCE, HOW A MISSION IS COMPLETED USUALLY DEFINES ITS LEVEL OF SUCCESS.
NO OFFENSE, GENERAL, BUT THAT SOUNDS LIKE THE TALK OF A PEACEMAKER --

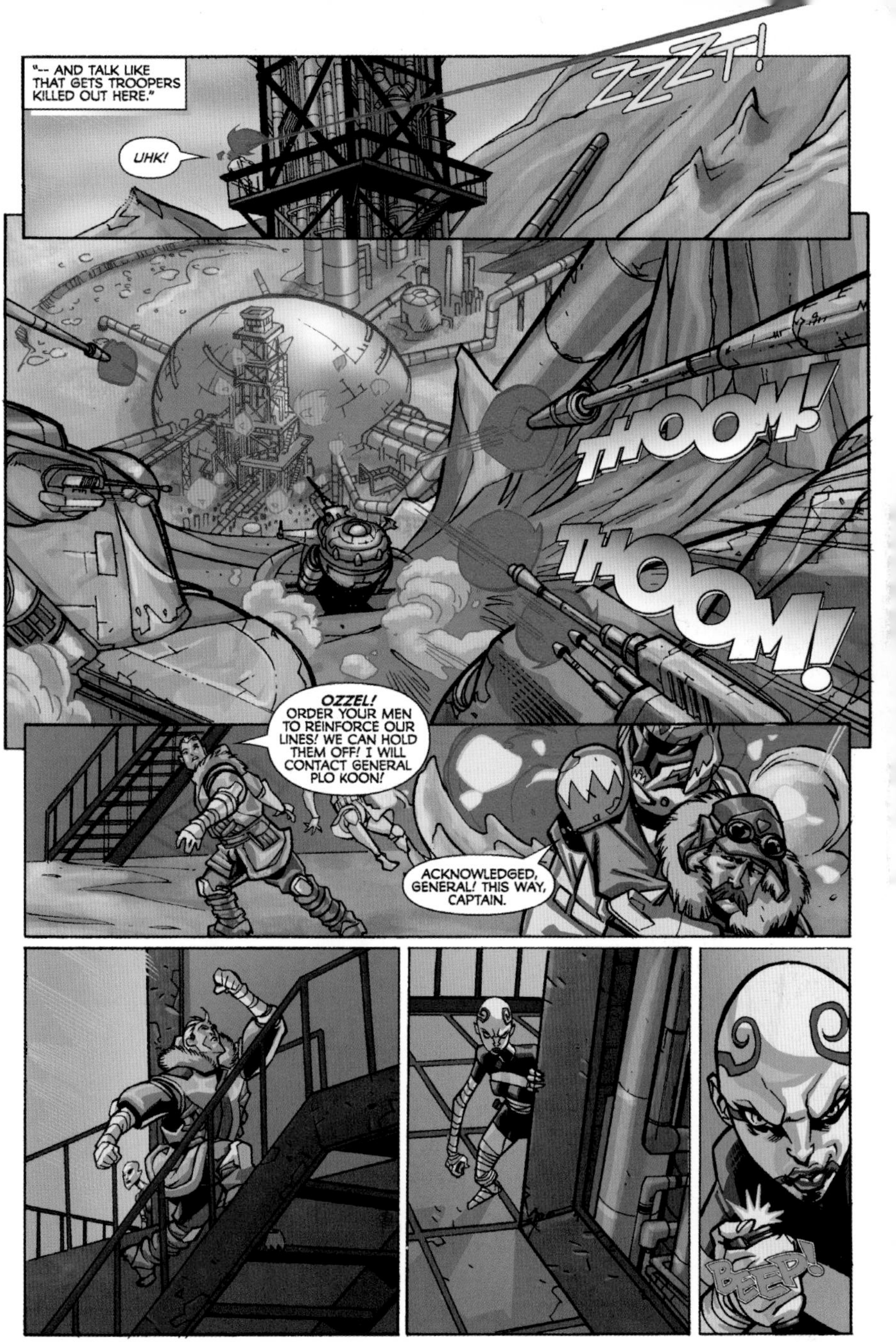

"-- AND TALK LIKE THAT GETS TROOPERS KILLED OUT HERE."
ZZZZT!
UHK!
THOOM!
THOOM!
OZZEL! ORDER YOUR MEN TO REINFORCE OUR LINES! WE CAN HOLD THEM OFF! I WILL CONTACT GENERAL PLO KOON!
ACKNOWLEDGED, GENERAL! THIS WAY, CAPTAIN.
BEEP!

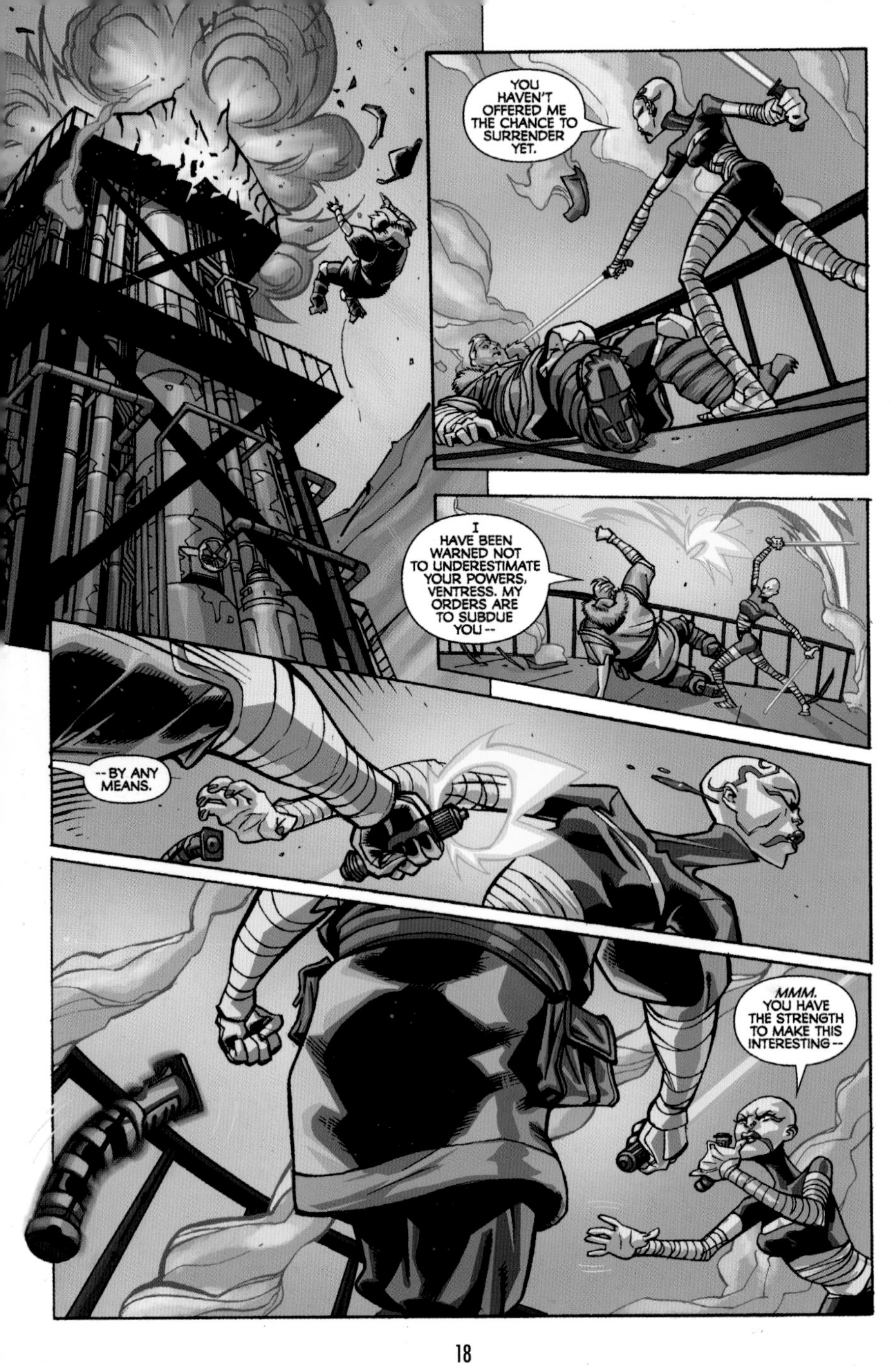
YOU HAVEN'T OFFERED ME THE CHANCE TO SURRENDER YET.
I HAVE BEEN WARNED NOT TO UNDERESTIMATE YOUR POWERS, VENTRESS. MY ORDERS ARE TO SUBDUE YOU --
-- BY ANY MEANS.
MMM. YOU HAVE THE STRENGTH TO MAKE THIS INTERESTING --

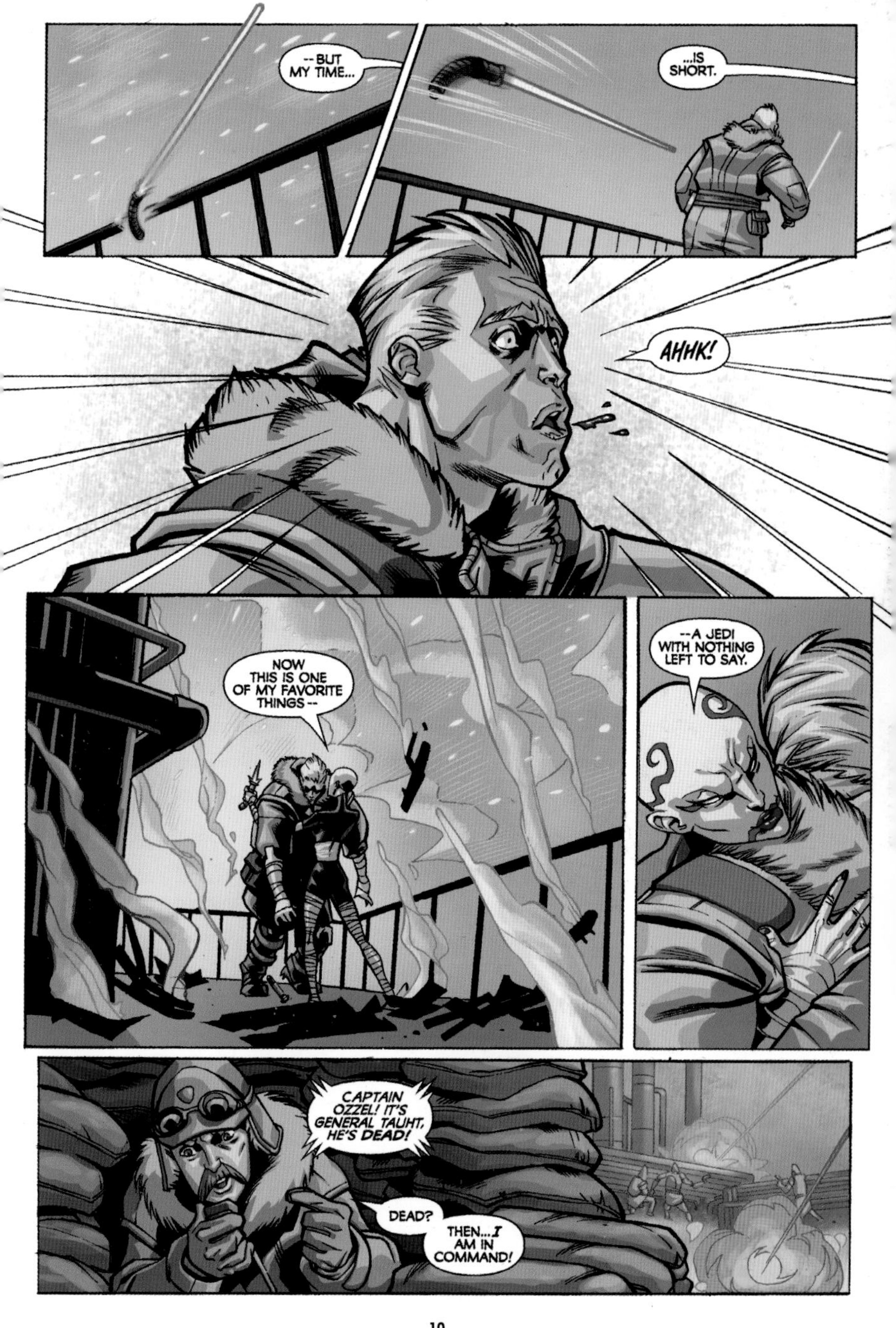
-- BUT MY TIME...
...IS SHORT.
AHHK!
NOW THIS IS ONE OF MY FAVORITE THINGS --
--A JEDI WITH NOTHING LEFT TO SAY.
CAPTAIN OZZEL! IT'S GENERAL TAUHT, HE'S DEAD!
DEAD?
THEN...I AM IN COMMAND!

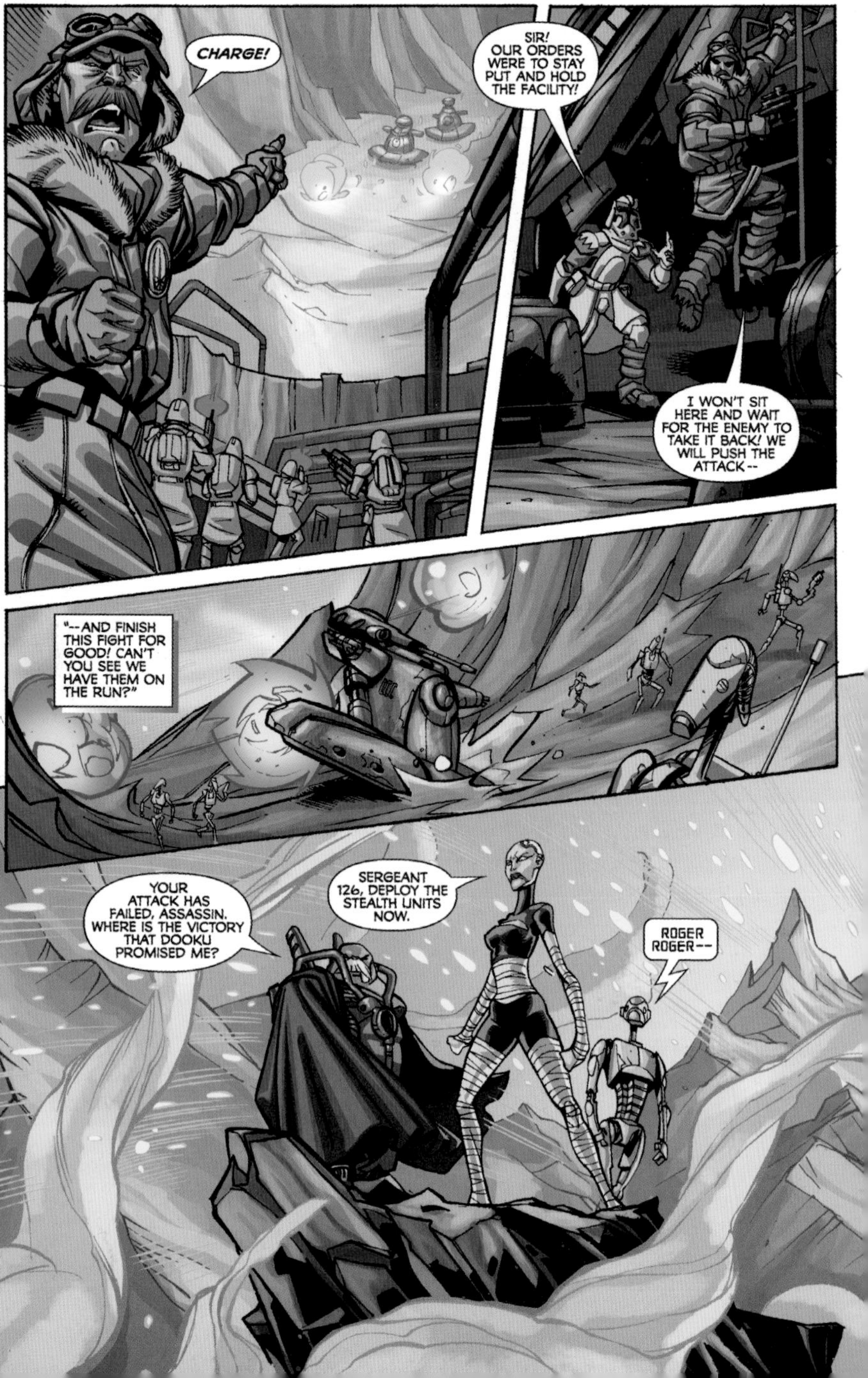
CHARGE!
SIR! OUR ORDERS WERE TO STAY PUT AND HOLD THE FACILITY!
I WON'T SIT HERE AND WAIT FOR THE ENEMY TO TAKE IT BACK! WE WILL PUSH THE ATTACK--
"--AND FINISH THIS FIGHT FOR GOOD! CAN'T YOU SEE WE HAVE THEM ON THE RUN?"
YOUR ATTACK HAS FAILED, ASSASSIN. WHERE IS THE VICTORY THAT DOOKU PROMISED ME?
SERGEANT 126, DEPLOY THE STEALTH UNITS NOW.
ROGER ROGER--

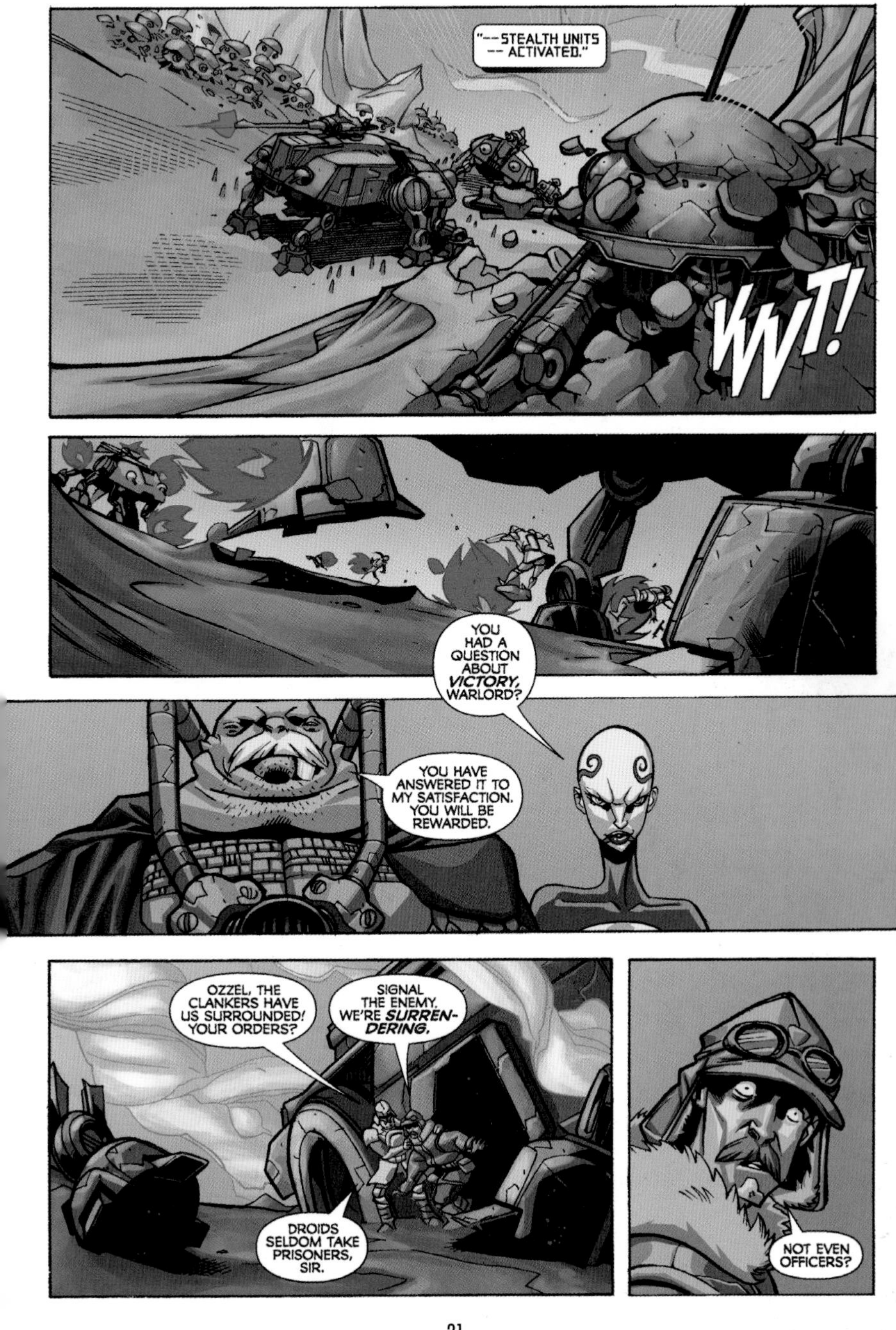
"--STEALTH UNITS
-- ACTIVATED."
KWT!
YOU HAD A QUESTION ABOUT *VICTORY,* WARLORD?
YOU HAVE ANSWERED IT TO MY SATISFACTION. YOU WILL BE REWARDED.
OZZEL, THE CLANKERS HAVE US SURROUNDED! YOUR ORDERS?
SIGNAL THE ENEMY. WE'RE *SURREN-DERING.*
DROIDS SELDOM TAKE PRISONERS, SIR.
NOT EVEN OFFICERS?

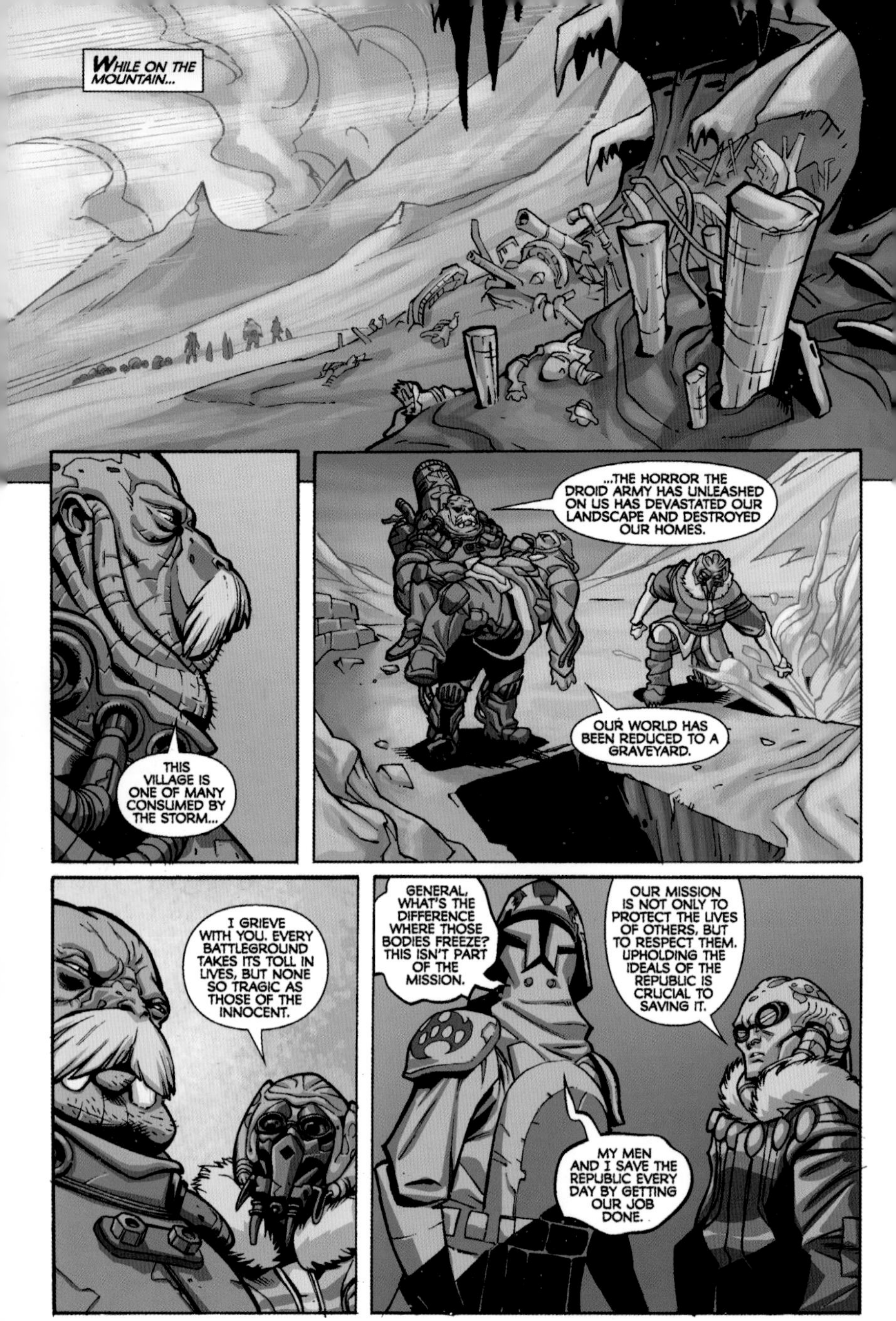
WHILE ON THE MOUNTAIN...
THIS VILLAGE IS ONE OF MANY CONSUMED BY THE STORM...
...THE HORROR THE DROID ARMY HAS UNLEASHED ON US HAS DEVASTATED OUR LANDSCAPE AND DESTROYED OUR HOMES.
OUR WORLD HAS BEEN REDUCED TO A GRAVEYARD.
I GRIEVE WITH YOU. EVERY BATTLEGROUND TAKES ITS TOLL IN LIVES, BUT NONE SO TRAGIC AS THOSE OF THE INNOCENT.
GENERAL, WHAT'S THE DIFFERENCE WHERE THOSE BODIES FREEZE? THIS ISN'T PART OF THE MISSION.
OUR MISSION IS NOT ONLY TO PROTECT THE LIVES OF OTHERS, BUT TO RESPECT THEM. UPHOLDING THE IDEALS OF THE REPUBLIC IS CRUCIAL TO SAVING IT.
MY MEN AND I SAVE THE REPUBLIC EVERY DAY BY GETTING OUR JOB DONE.

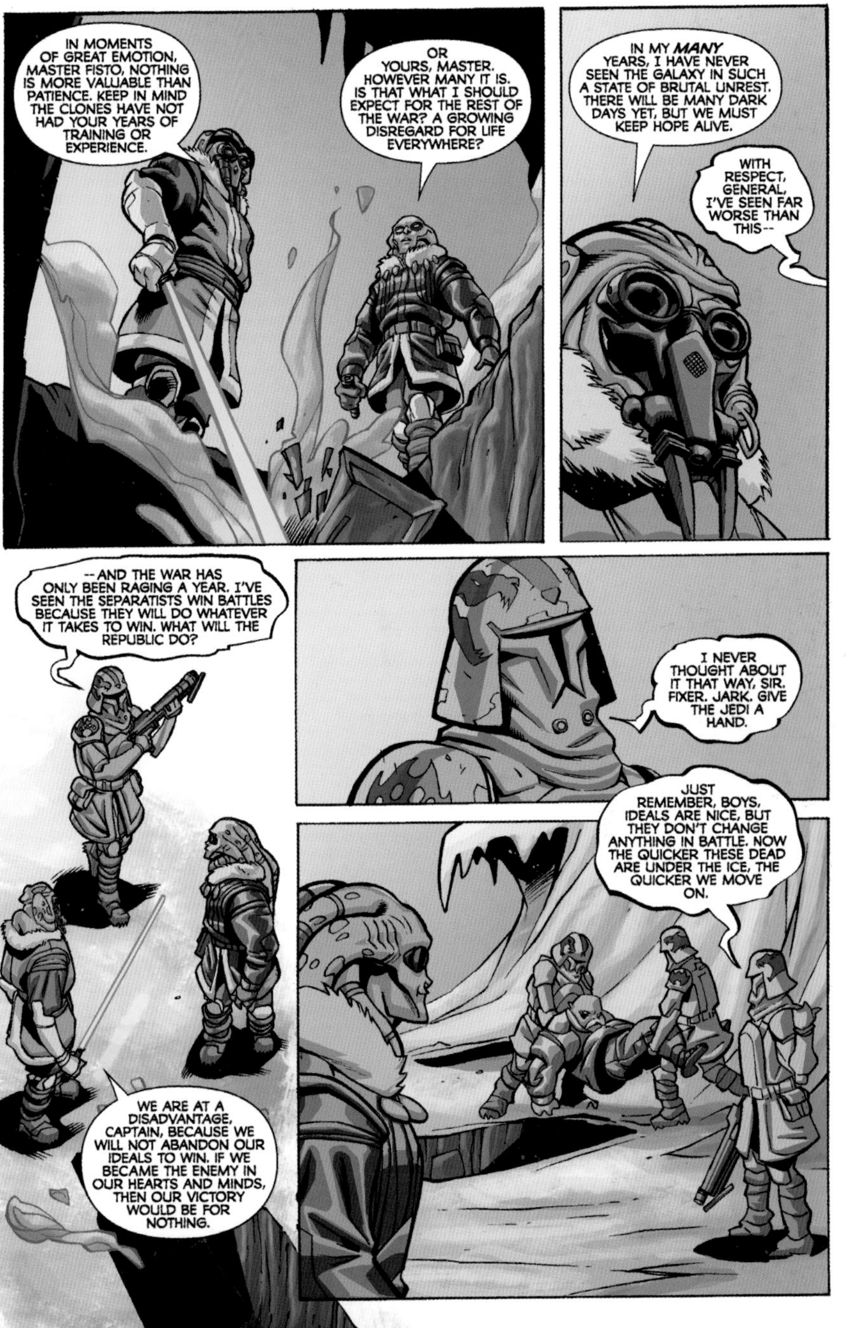

IN MOMENTS OF GREAT EMOTION, MASTER FISTO, NOTHING IS MORE VALUABLE THAN PATIENCE. KEEP IN MIND THE CLONES HAVE NOT HAD YOUR YEARS OF TRAINING OR EXPERIENCE.
OR YOURS, MASTER. HOWEVER MANY IT IS. IS THAT WHAT I SHOULD EXPECT FOR THE REST OF THE WAR? A GROWING DISREGARD FOR LIFE EVERYWHERE?
IN MY *MANY* YEARS, I HAVE NEVER SEEN THE GALAXY IN SUCH A STATE OF BRUTAL UNREST. THERE WILL BE MANY DARK DAYS YET, BUT WE MUST KEEP HOPE ALIVE.
WITH RESPECT, GENERAL, I'VE SEEN FAR WORSE THAN THIS--
--AND THE WAR HAS ONLY BEEN RAGING A YEAR. I'VE SEEN THE SEPARATISTS WIN BATTLES BECAUSE THEY WILL DO WHATEVER IT TAKES TO WIN. WHAT WILL THE REPUBLIC DO?
WE ARE AT A DISADVANTAGE, CAPTAIN, BECAUSE WE WILL NOT ABANDON OUR IDEALS TO WIN. IF WE BECAME THE ENEMY IN OUR HEARTS AND MINDS, THEN OUR VICTORY WOULD BE FOR NOTHING.
I NEVER THOUGHT ABOUT IT THAT WAY, SIR. FIXER. JARK. GIVE THE JEDI A HAND.
JUST REMEMBER, BOYS, IDEALS ARE NICE, BUT THEY DON'T CHANGE ANYTHING IN BATTLE. NOW THE QUICKER THESE DEAD ARE UNDER THE ICE, THE QUICKER WE MOVE ON.

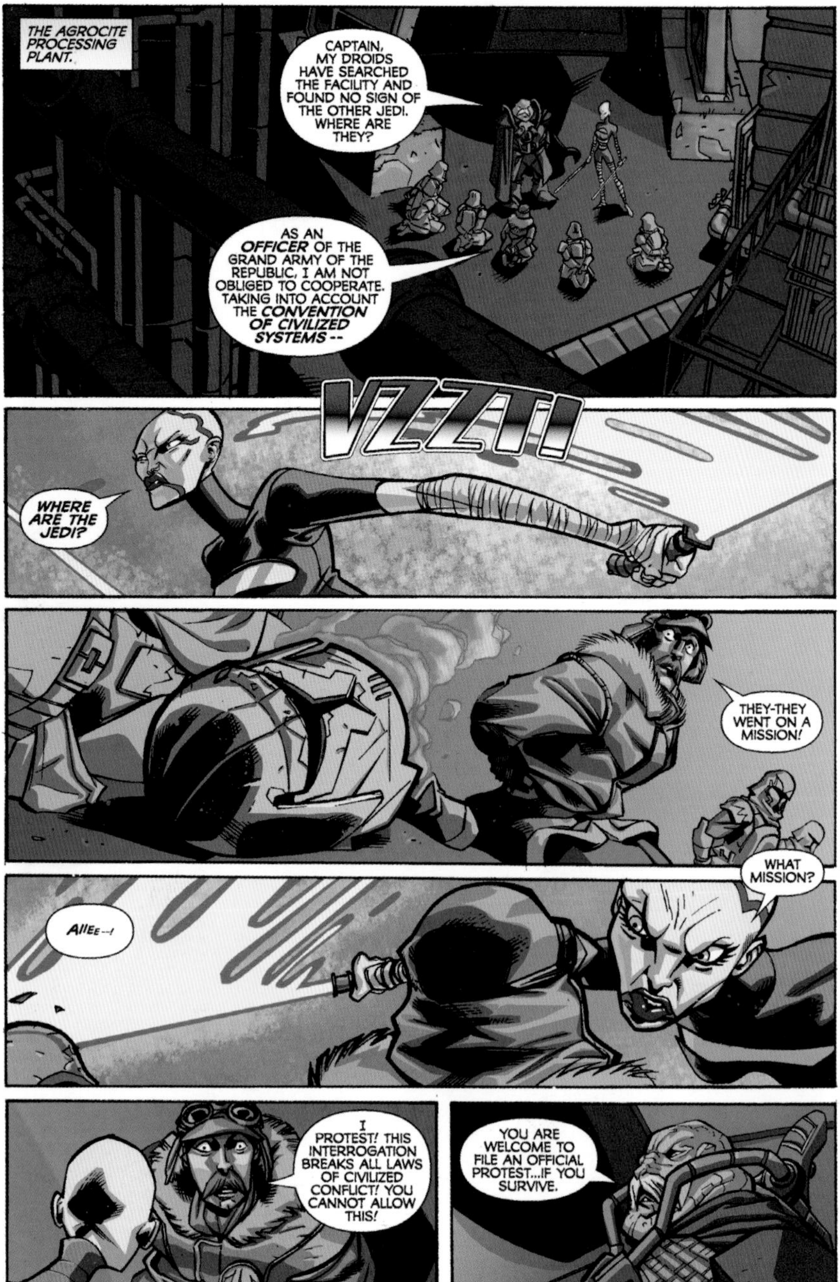
THE AGROCITE PROCESSING PLANT.
CAPTAIN, MY DROIDS HAVE SEARCHED THE FACILITY AND FOUND NO SIGN OF THE OTHER JEDI. WHERE ARE THEY?
AS AN OFFICER OF THE GRAND ARMY OF THE REPUBLIC, I AM NOT OBLIGED TO COOPERATE. TAKING INTO ACCOUNT THE CONVENTION OF CIVILIZED SYSTEMS --
VZZZT!
WHERE ARE THE JEDI?
THEY-THEY WENT ON A MISSION!
WHAT MISSION?
AIIEE--!
I PROTEST! THIS INTERROGATION BREAKS ALL LAWS OF CIVILIZED CONFLICT! YOU CANNOT ALLOW THIS!
YOU ARE WELCOME TO FILE AN OFFICIAL PROTEST...IF YOU SURVIVE.

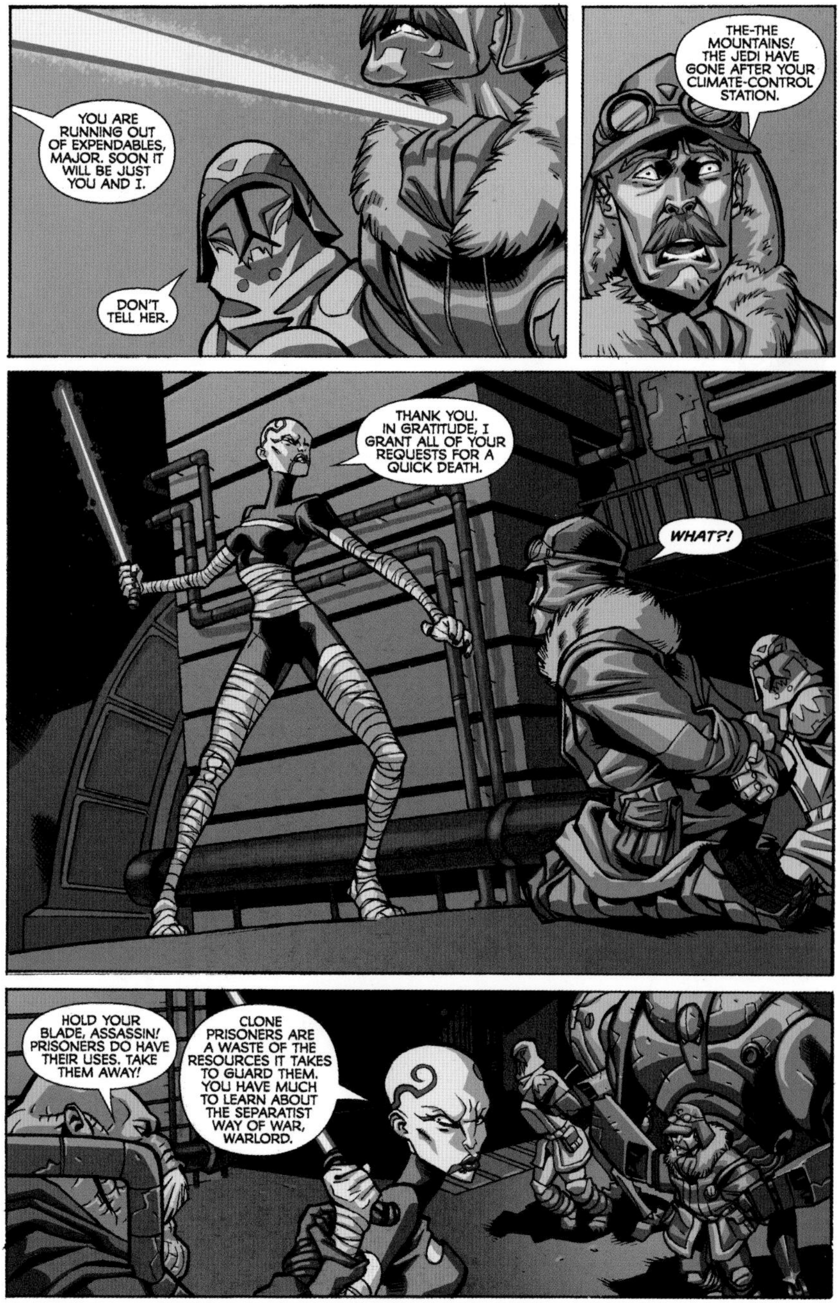
YOU ARE RUNNING OUT OF EXPENDABLES, MAJOR. SOON IT WILL BE JUST YOU AND I.
DON'T TELL HER.
THE-THE MOUNTAINS! THE JEDI HAVE GONE AFTER YOUR CLIMATE-CONTROL STATION.
THANK YOU. IN GRATITUDE, I GRANT ALL OF YOUR REQUESTS FOR A QUICK DEATH.
WHAT?!
HOLD YOUR BLADE, ASSASSIN! PRISONERS DO HAVE THEIR USES. TAKE THEM AWAY!
CLONE PRISONERS ARE A WASTE OF THE RESOURCES IT TAKES TO GUARD THEM. YOU HAVE MUCH TO LEARN ABOUT THE SEPARATIST WAY OF WAR, WARLORD.

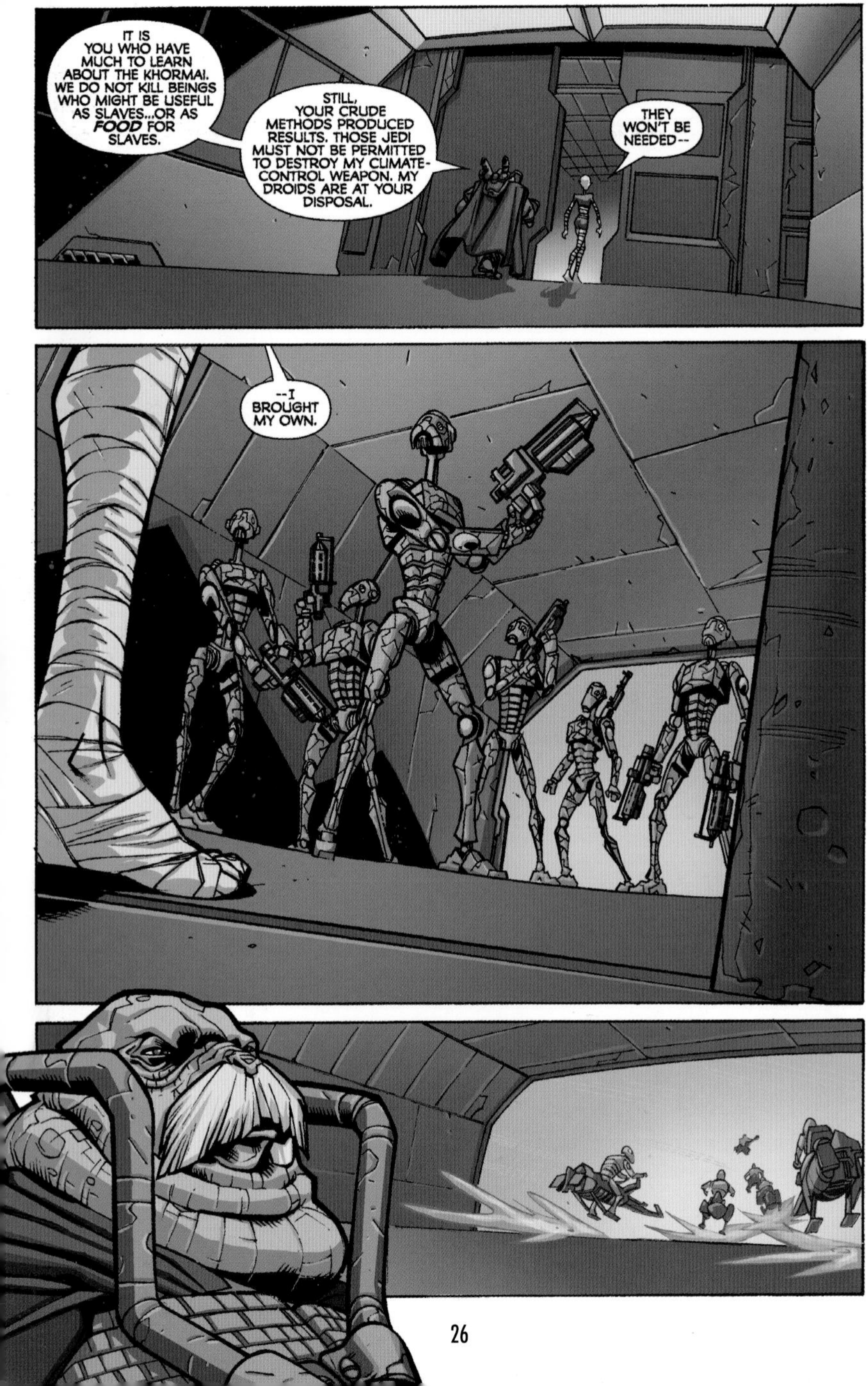
IT IS YOU WHO HAVE MUCH TO LEARN ABOUT THE KHORMAI. WE DO NOT KILL BEINGS WHO MIGHT BE USEFUL AS SLAVES...OR AS *FOOD* FOR SLAVES.
STILL, YOUR CRUDE METHODS PRODUCED RESULTS. THOSE JEDI MUST NOT BE PERMITTED TO DESTROY MY CLIMATE-CONTROL WEAPON. MY DROIDS ARE AT YOUR DISPOSAL.
THEY WON'T BE NEEDED--
--I BROUGHT MY OWN.

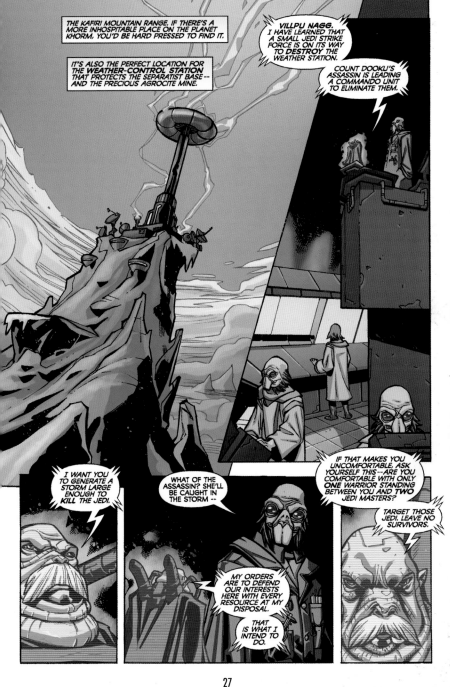

THE KAFIRI MOUNTAIN RANGE. IF THERE'S A MORE INHOSPITABLE PLACE ON THE PLANET KHORM, YOU'D BE HARD PRESSED TO FIND IT.

IT'S ALSO THE PERFECT LOCATION FOR THE WEATHER-CONTROL STATION THAT PROTECTS THE SEPARATIST BASE -- AND THE PRECIOUS AGROCITE MINE.

VILLPU NAGG. I HAVE LEARNED THAT A SMALL JEDI STRIKE FORCE IS ON ITS WAY TO DESTROY THE WEATHER STATION.

COUNT DOOKU'S ASSASSIN IS LEADING A COMMANDO UNIT TO ELIMINATE THEM.

IF THAT MAKES YOU UNCOMFORTABLE, ASK YOURSELF THIS -- ARE YOU COMFORTABLE WITH ONLY ONE WARRIOR STANDING BETWEEN YOU AND TWO JEDI MASTERS?

I WANT YOU TO GENERATE A STORM LARGE ENOUGH TO KILL THE JEDI.

WHAT OF THE ASSASSIN? SHE'LL BE CAUGHT IN THE STORM --

TARGET THOSE JEDI. LEAVE NO SURVIVORS.

MY ORDERS ARE TO DEFEND OUR INTERESTS HERE WITH EVERY RESOURCE AT MY DISPOSAL.

THAT IS WHAT I INTEND TO DO.

27

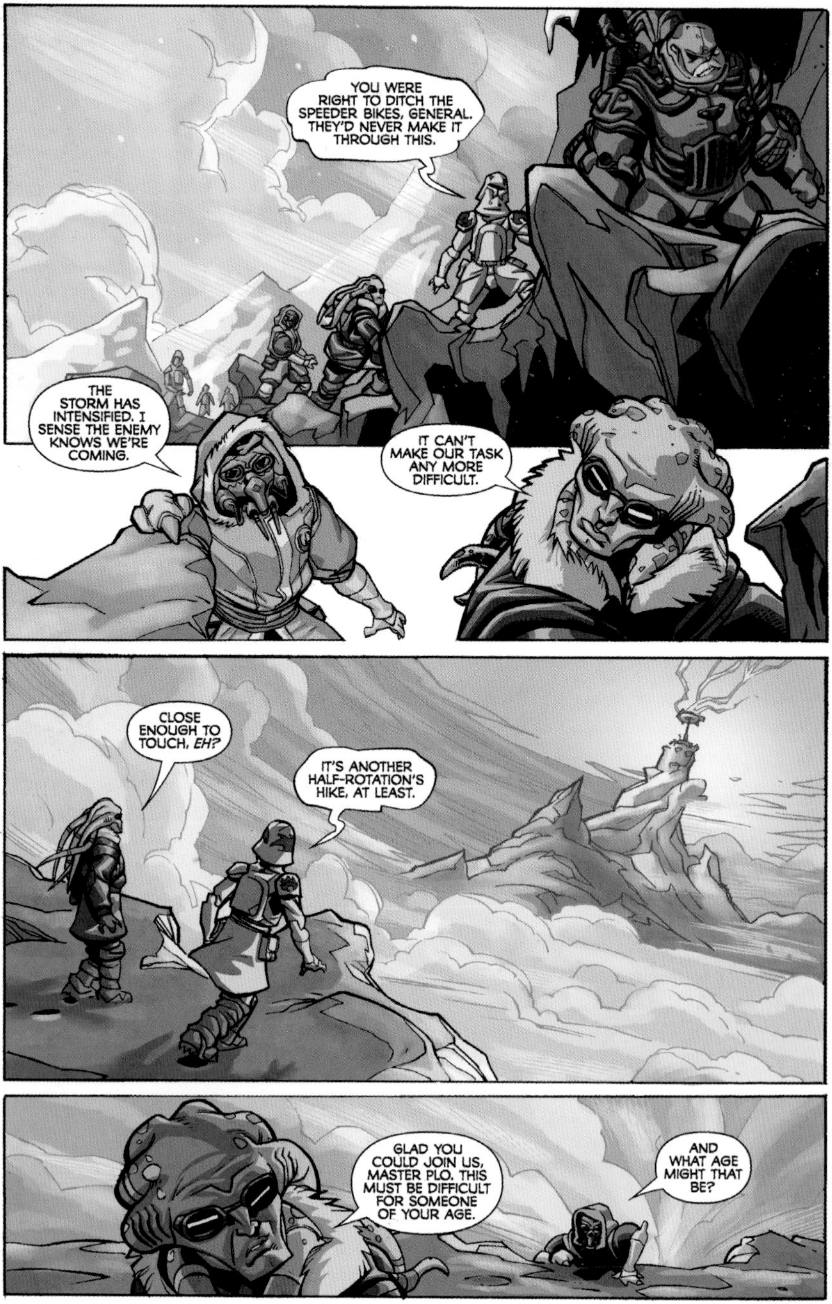
YOU WERE RIGHT TO DITCH THE SPEEDER BIKES, GENERAL. THEY'D NEVER MAKE IT THROUGH THIS.
THE STORM HAS INTENSIFIED. I SENSE THE ENEMY KNOWS WE'RE COMING.
IT CAN'T MAKE OUR TASK ANY MORE DIFFICULT.
CLOSE ENOUGH TO TOUCH, *EH?*
IT'S ANOTHER HALF-ROTATION'S HIKE, AT LEAST.
GLAD YOU COULD JOIN US, MASTER PLO. THIS MUST BE DIFFICULT FOR SOMEONE OF YOUR AGE.
AND WHAT AGE MIGHT THAT BE?

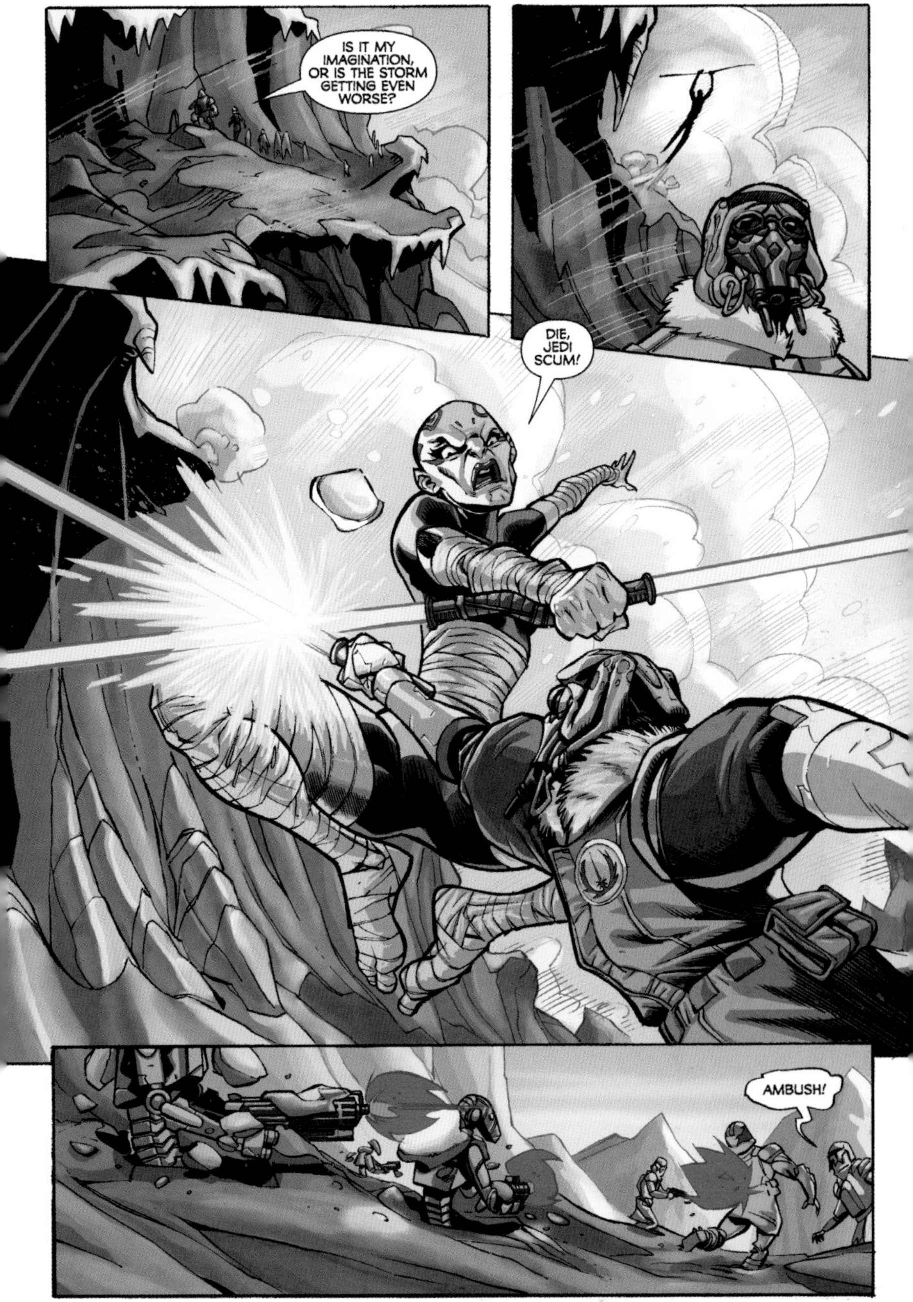
IS IT MY IMAGINATION, OR IS THE STORM GETTING EVEN WORSE?
DIE, JEDI SCUM!
AMBUSH!

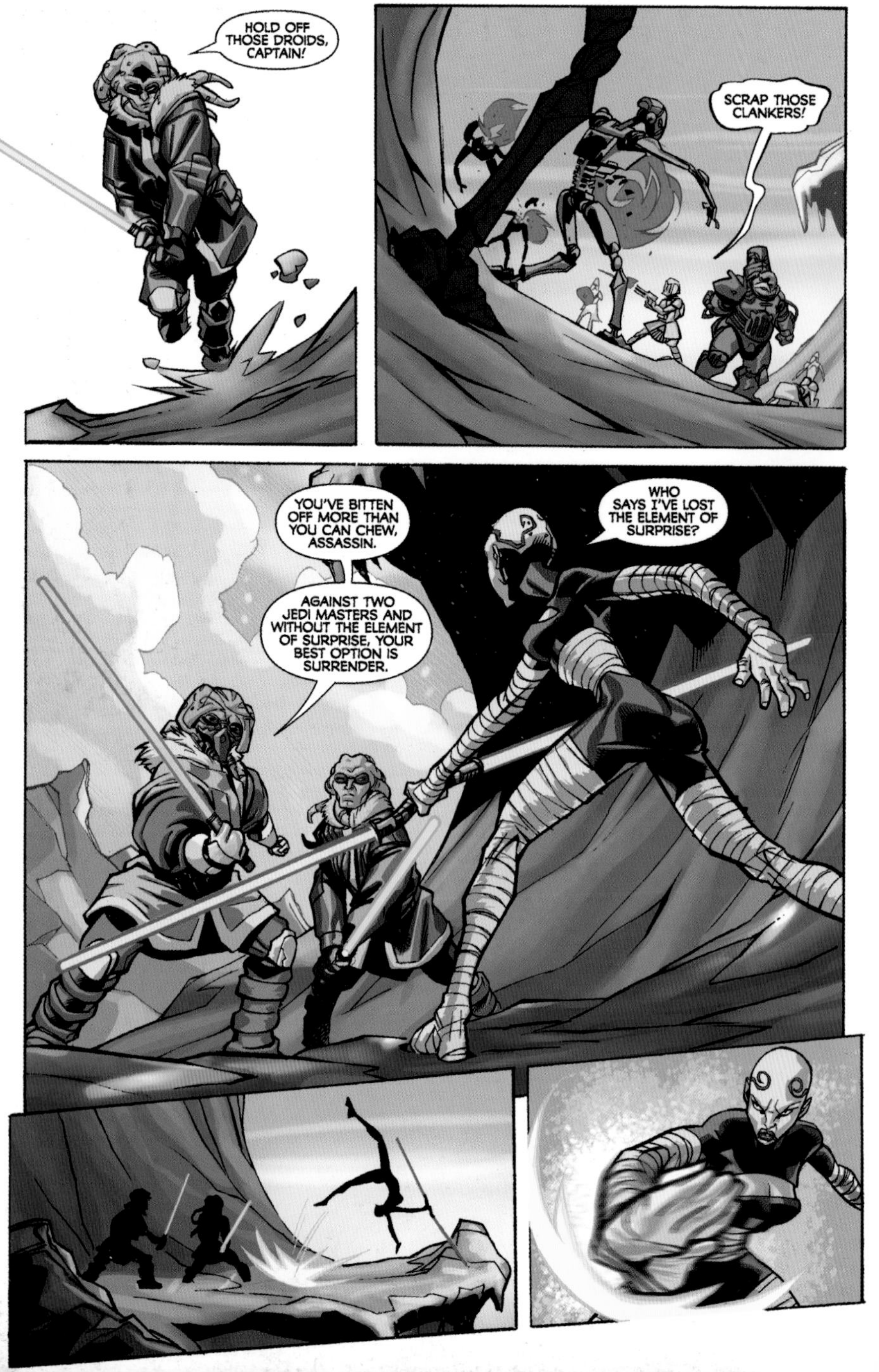
HOLD OFF THOSE DROIDS, CAPTAIN!
SCRAP THOSE CLANKERS!
YOU'VE BITTEN OFF MORE THAN YOU CAN CHEW, ASSASSIN.
AGAINST TWO JEDI MASTERS AND WITHOUT THE ELEMENT OF SURPRISE, YOUR BEST OPTION IS SURRENDER.
WHO SAYS I'VE LOST THE ELEMENT OF SURPRISE?

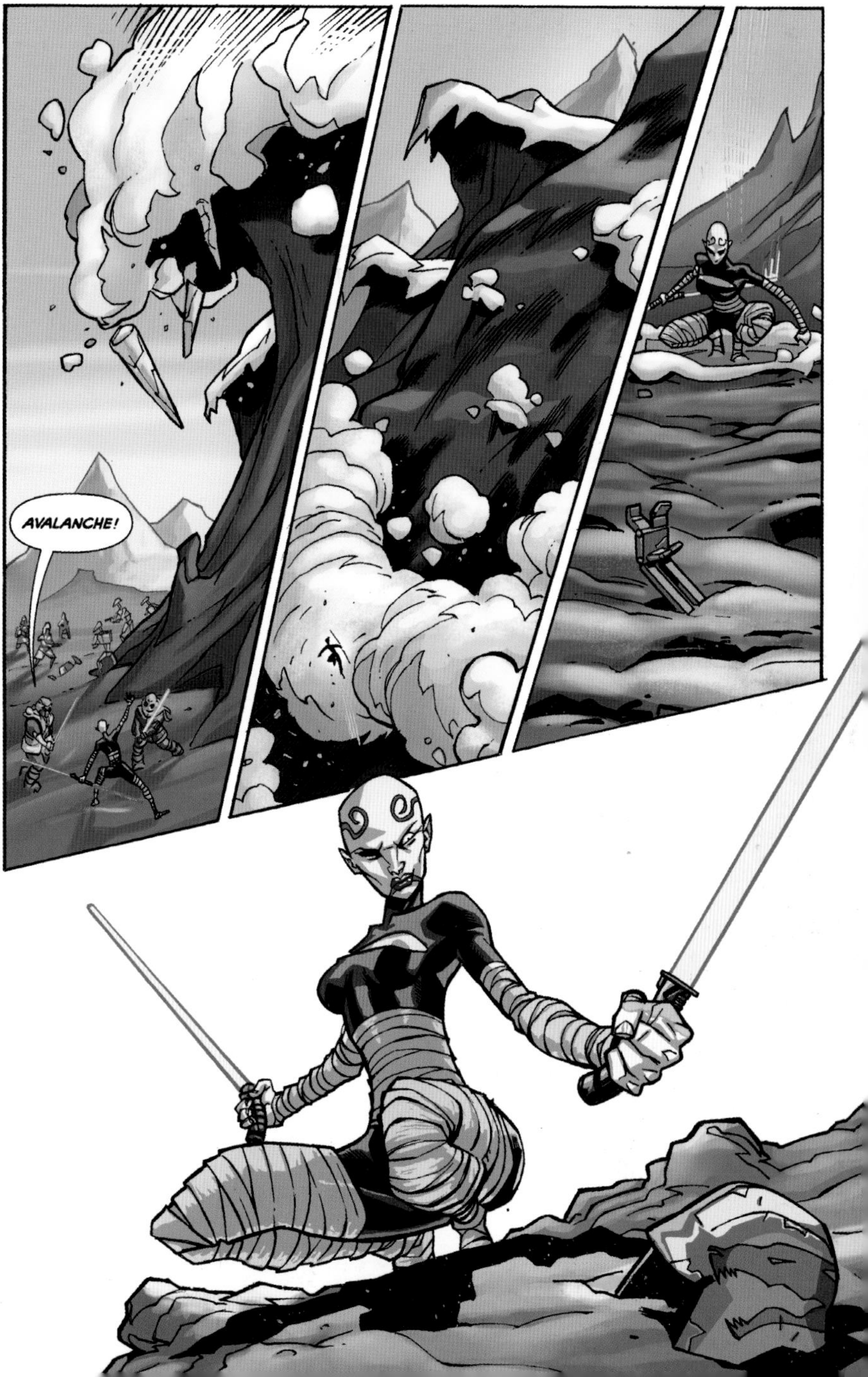
AVALANCHE!

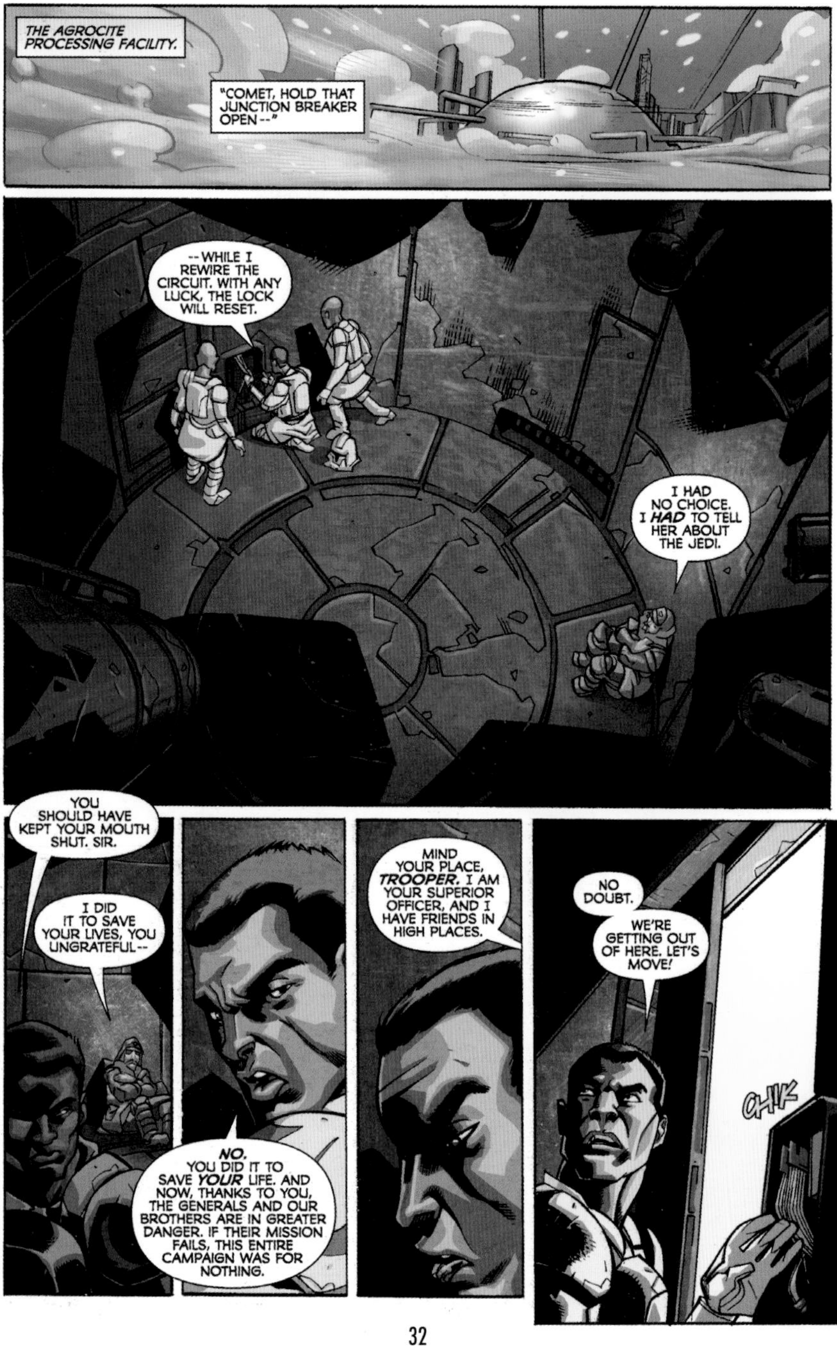
THE AGROCITE PROCESSING FACILITY.
"COMET, HOLD THAT JUNCTION BREAKER OPEN --"
--WHILE I REWIRE THE CIRCUIT. WITH ANY LUCK, THE LOCK WILL RESET.
I HAD NO CHOICE. I HAD TO TELL HER ABOUT THE JEDI.
YOU SHOULD HAVE KEPT YOUR MOUTH SHUT. SIR.
I DID IT TO SAVE YOUR LIVES, YOU UNGRATEFUL--
NO. YOU DID IT TO SAVE YOUR LIFE. AND NOW, THANKS TO YOU, THE GENERALS AND OUR BROTHERS ARE IN GREATER DANGER. IF THEIR MISSION FAILS, THIS ENTIRE CAMPAIGN WAS FOR NOTHING.
MIND YOUR PLACE, TROOPER. I AM YOUR SUPERIOR OFFICER, AND I HAVE FRIENDS IN HIGH PLACES.
NO DOUBT.
WE'RE GETTING OUT OF HERE. LET'S MOVE!
CHIK

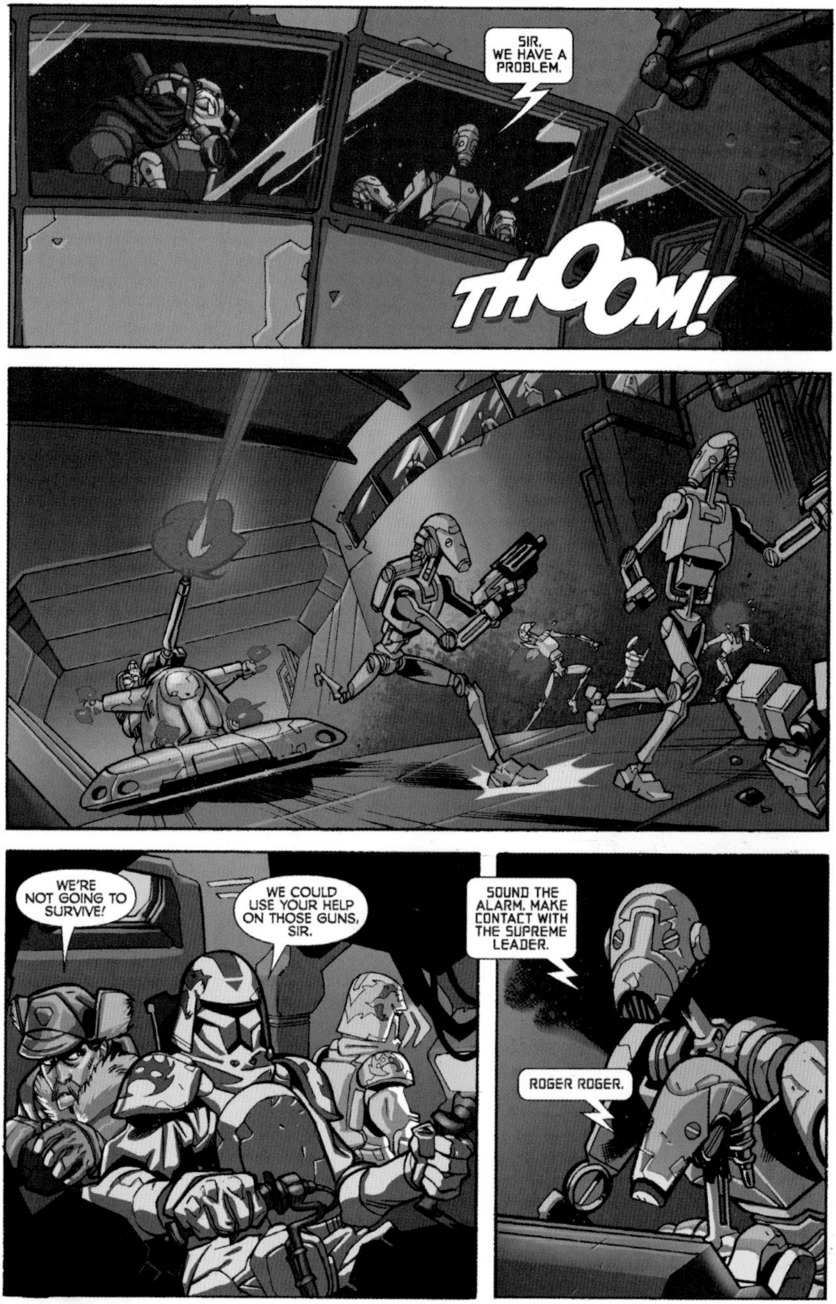
SIR, WE HAVE A PROBLEM.
THOOM!
WE'RE NOT GOING TO SURVIVE!
WE COULD USE YOUR HELP ON THOSE GUNS, SIR.
SOUND THE ALARM. MAKE CONTACT WITH THE SUPREME LEADER.
ROGER ROGER.

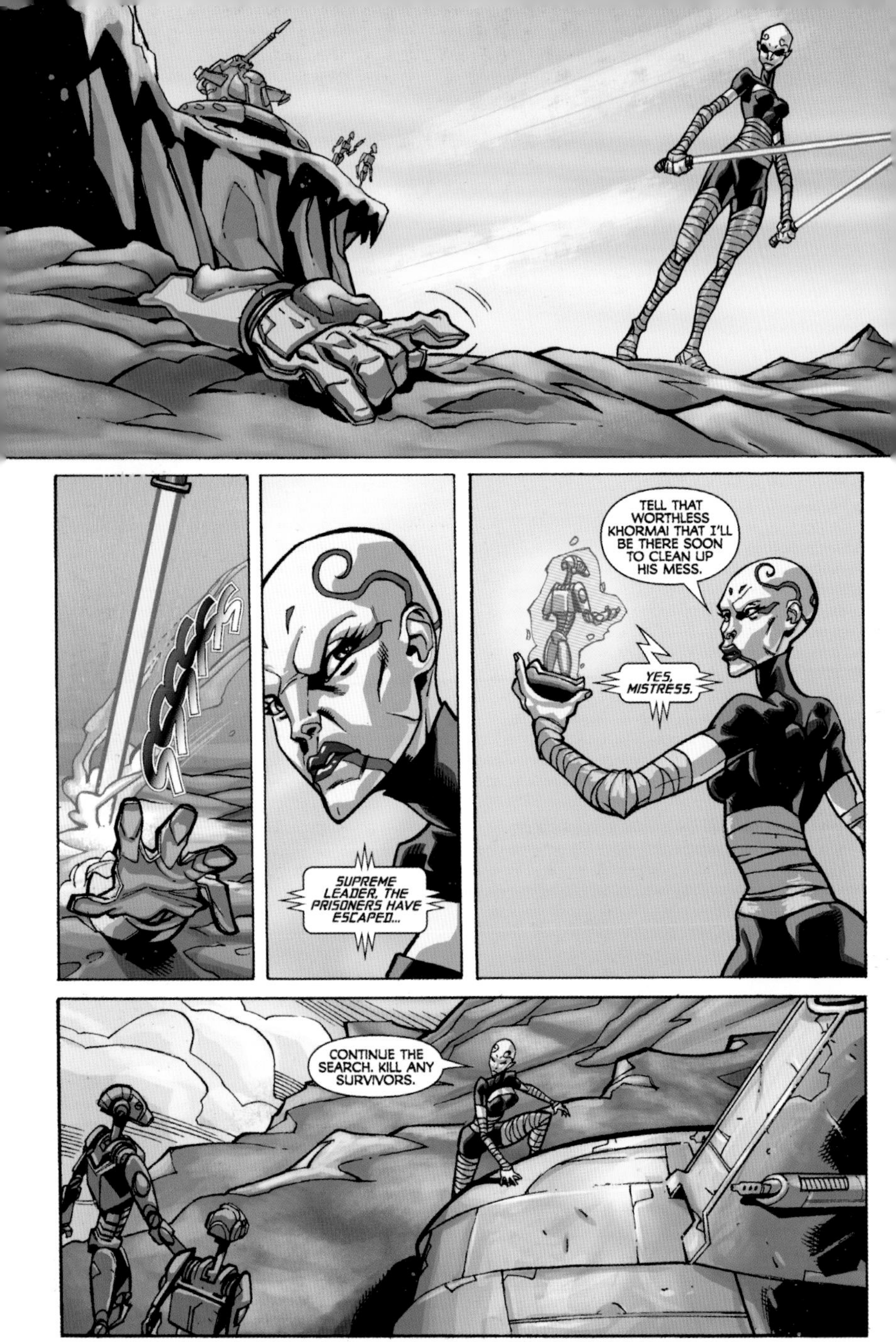

SUPREME LEADER, THE PRISONERS HAVE ESCAPED...
TELL THAT WORTHLESS KHORMAI THAT I'LL BE THERE SOON TO CLEAN UP HIS MESS.
YES, MISTRESS.
CONTINUE THE SEARCH. KILL ANY SURVIVORS.

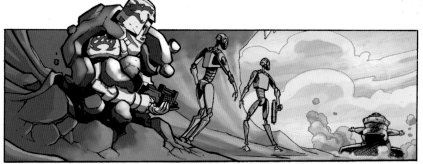

BOOM!

I DON'T KNOW HOW WE SURVIVED THAT ONE.

WE USED THE FORCE TO CREATE A POCKET THAT OFFERED SOME PROTECTION.

HOW IS YOUR ARM, MASTER PLO?

BROKEN. BONES BRITTLE WITH THE PASSING OF AGES.

WE LOST STEN, DEADEYE, BLUNT, AND JARK. AND WORSE--THE EXPLOSIVES ARE GONE.

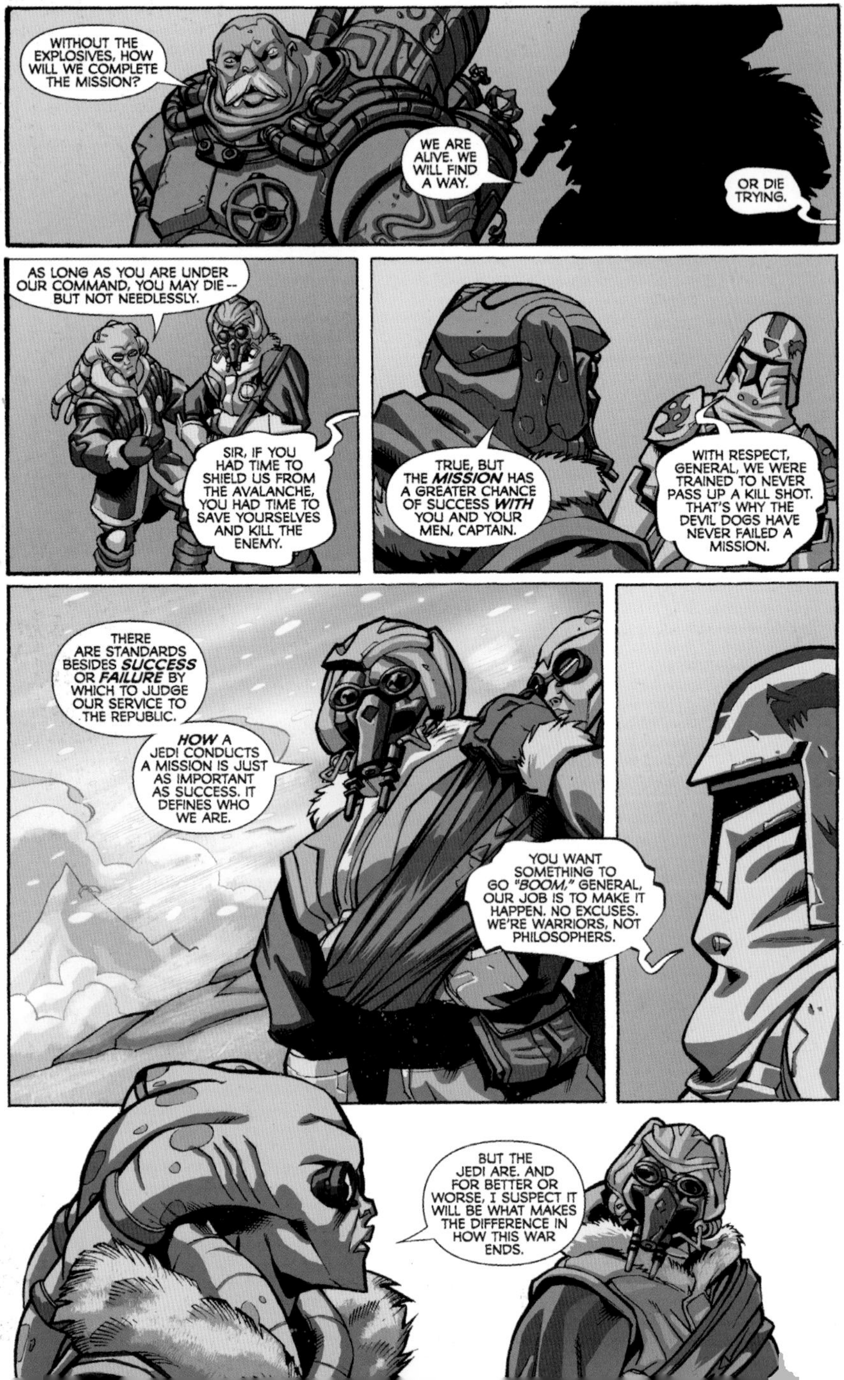
WITHOUT THE EXPLOSIVES, HOW WILL WE COMPLETE THE MISSION?
WE ARE ALIVE. WE WILL FIND A WAY.
OR DIE TRYING.
AS LONG AS YOU ARE UNDER OUR COMMAND, YOU MAY DIE-- BUT NOT NEEDLESSLY.
SIR, IF YOU HAD TIME TO SHIELD US FROM THE AVALANCHE, YOU HAD TIME TO SAVE YOURSELVES AND KILL THE ENEMY.
TRUE, BUT THE MISSION HAS A GREATER CHANCE OF SUCCESS WITH YOU AND YOUR MEN, CAPTAIN.
WITH RESPECT, GENERAL, WE WERE TRAINED TO NEVER PASS UP A KILL SHOT. THAT'S WHY THE DEVIL DOGS HAVE NEVER FAILED A MISSION.
THERE ARE STANDARDS BESIDES SUCCESS OR FAILURE BY WHICH TO JUDGE OUR SERVICE TO THE REPUBLIC.
HOW A JEDI CONDUCTS A MISSION IS JUST AS IMPORTANT AS SUCCESS. IT DEFINES WHO WE ARE.
YOU WANT SOMETHING TO GO "BOOM," GENERAL, OUR JOB IS TO MAKE IT HAPPEN. NO EXCUSES. WE'RE WARRIORS, NOT PHILOSOPHERS.
BUT THE JEDI ARE. AND FOR BETTER OR WORSE, I SUSPECT IT WILL BE WHAT MAKES THE DIFFERENCE IN HOW THIS WAR ENDS.

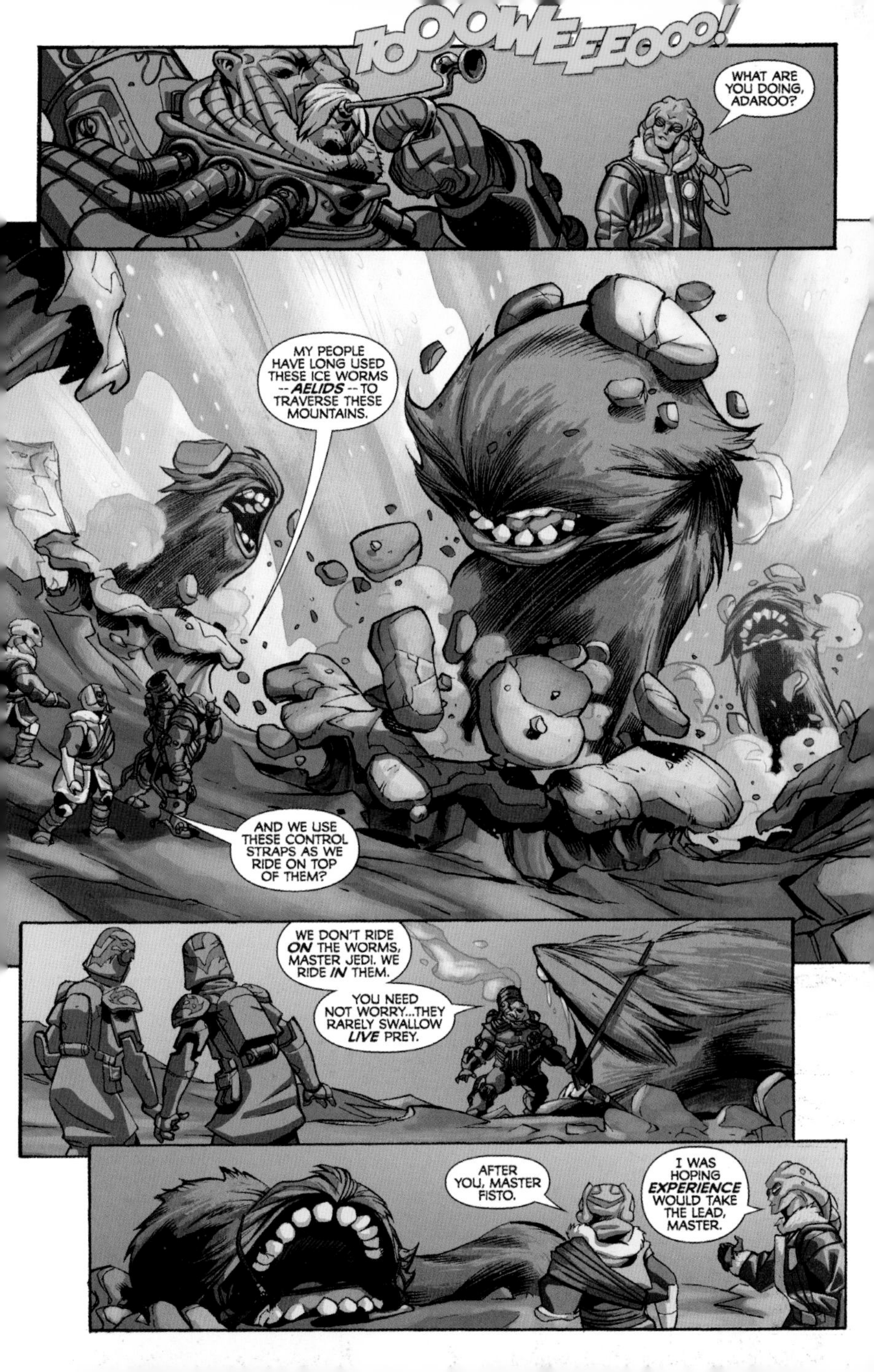
TOOOWEEEOOO!
WHAT ARE YOU DOING, ADAROO?
MY PEOPLE HAVE LONG USED THESE ICE WORMS --AELIDS-- TO TRAVERSE THESE MOUNTAINS.
AND WE USE THESE CONTROL STRAPS AS WE RIDE ON TOP OF THEM?
WE DON'T RIDE ON THE WORMS, MASTER JEDI. WE RIDE IN THEM.
YOU NEED NOT WORRY...THEY RARELY SWALLOW LIVE PREY.
AFTER YOU, MASTER FISTO.
I WAS HOPING EXPERIENCE WOULD TAKE THE LEAD, MASTER.

MEANWHILE...

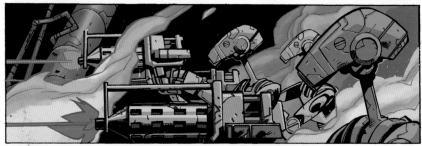

NOW'S OUR CHANCE!

GET US THROUGH THAT OPENING!

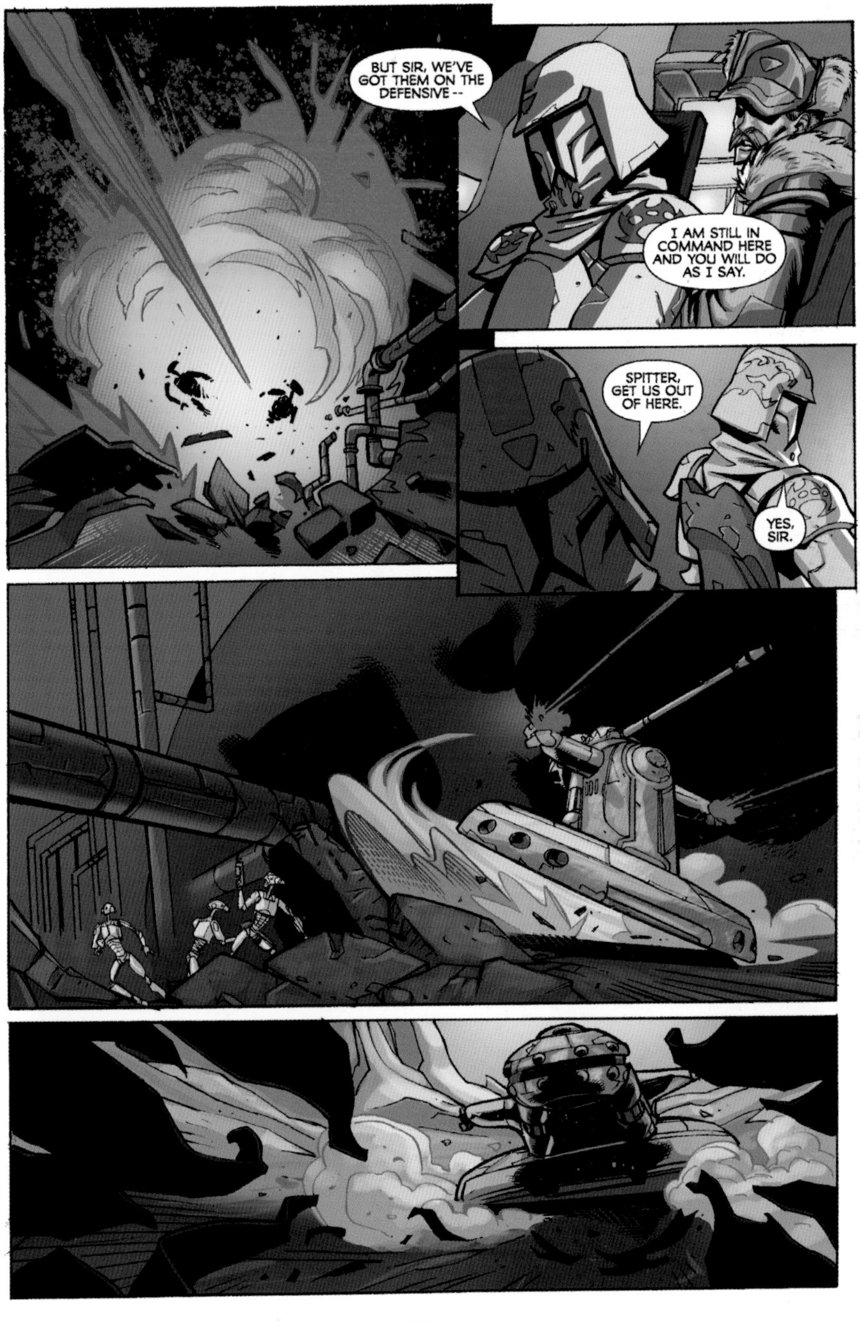
BUT SIR, WE'VE GOT THEM ON THE DEFENSIVE --
I AM STILL IN COMMAND HERE AND YOU WILL DO AS I SAY.
SPITTER, GET US OUT OF HERE.
YES, SIR.

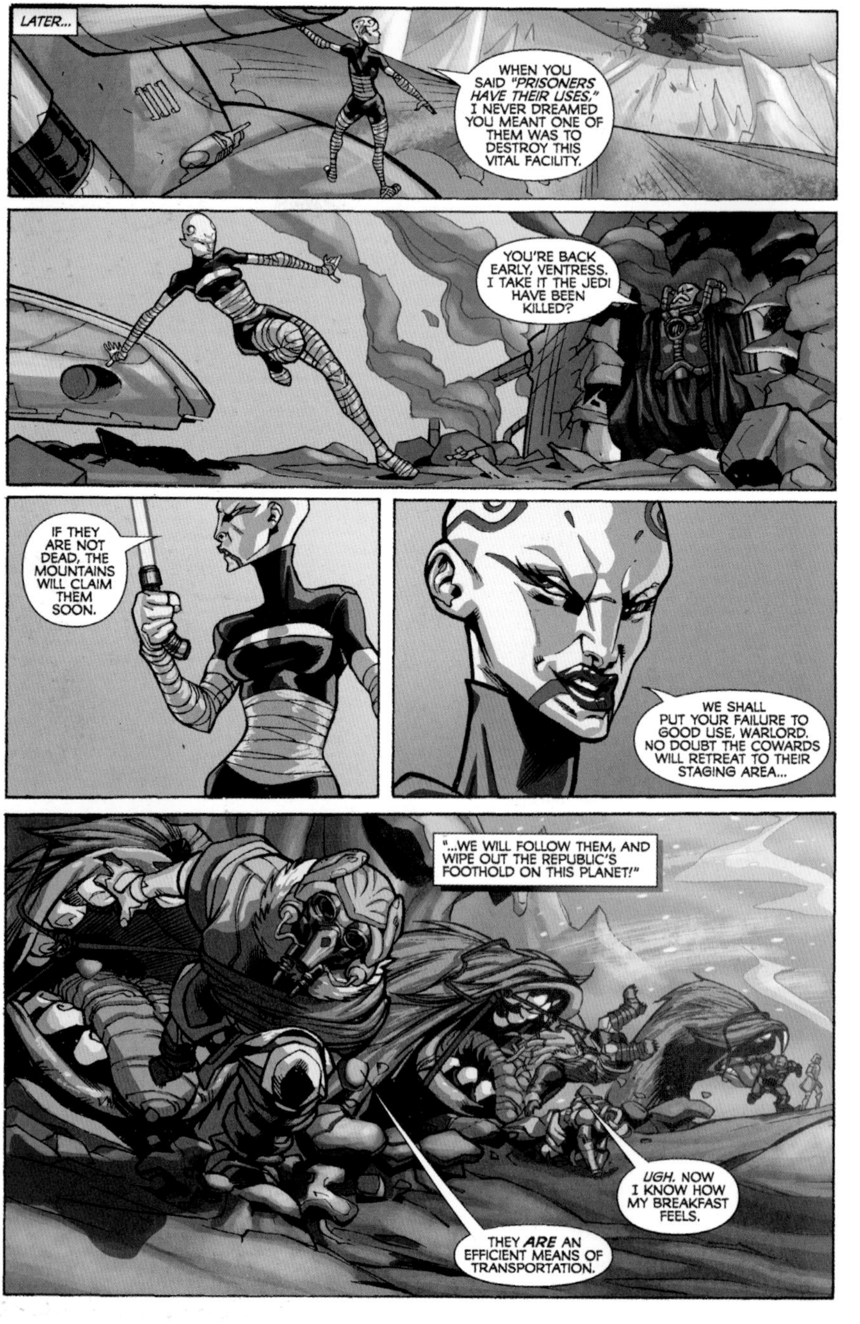
LATER...
WHEN YOU SAID "PRISONERS HAVE THEIR USES," I NEVER DREAMED YOU MEANT ONE OF THEM WAS TO DESTROY THIS VITAL FACILITY.
YOU'RE BACK EARLY, VENTRESS. I TAKE IT THE JEDI HAVE BEEN KILLED?
IF THEY ARE NOT DEAD, THE MOUNTAINS WILL CLAIM THEM SOON.
WE SHALL PUT YOUR FAILURE TO GOOD USE, WARLORD. NO DOUBT THE COWARDS WILL RETREAT TO THEIR STAGING AREA...
"...WE WILL FOLLOW THEM, AND WIPE OUT THE REPUBLIC'S FOOTHOLD ON THIS PLANET!"
UGH. NOW I KNOW HOW MY BREAKFAST FEELS.
THEY ARE AN EFFICIENT MEANS OF TRANSPORTATION.

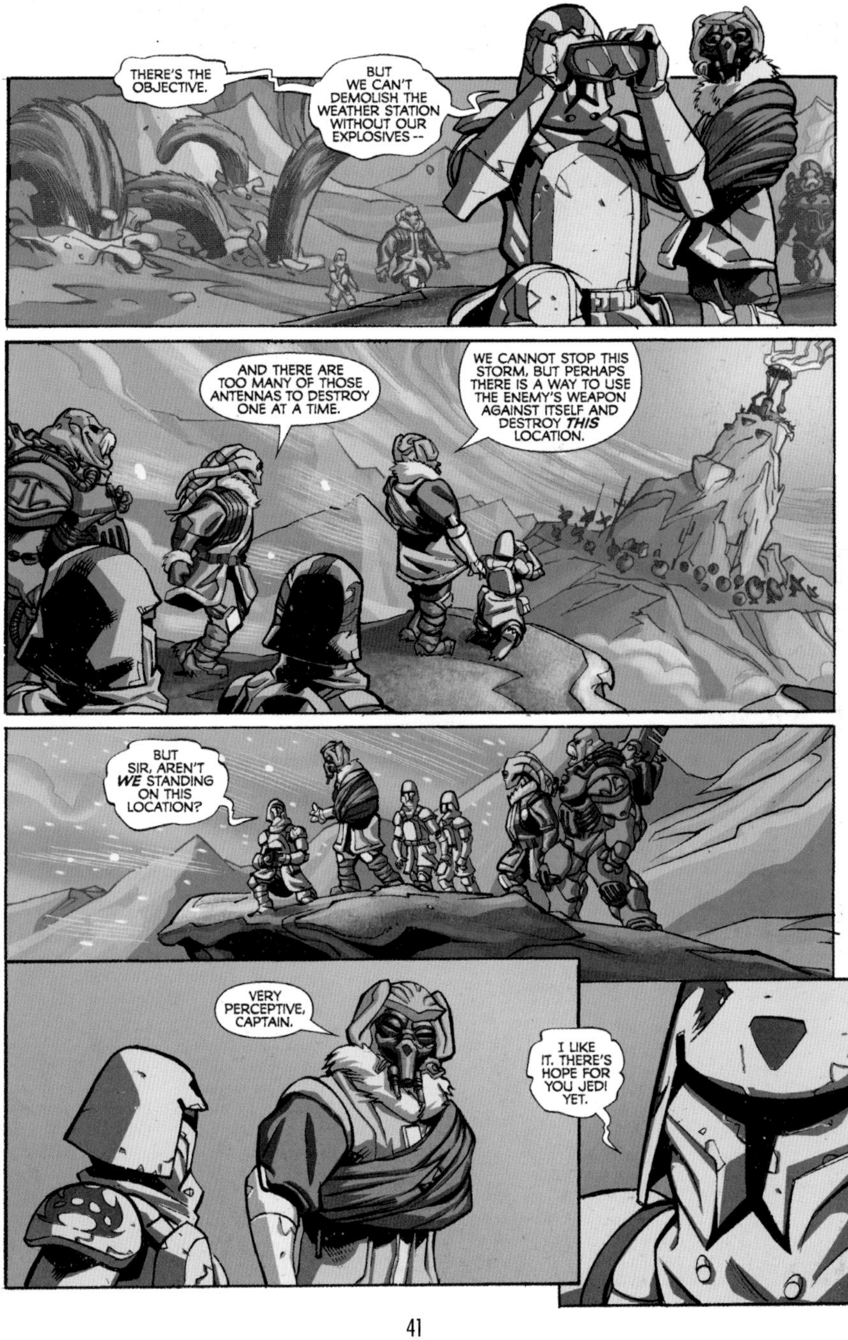
THERE'S THE OBJECTIVE.
BUT WE CAN'T DEMOLISH THE WEATHER STATION WITHOUT OUR EXPLOSIVES--
AND THERE ARE TOO MANY OF THOSE ANTENNAS TO DESTROY ONE AT A TIME.
WE CANNOT STOP THIS STORM, BUT PERHAPS THERE IS A WAY TO USE THE ENEMY'S WEAPON AGAINST ITSELF AND DESTROY *THIS* LOCATION.
BUT SIR, AREN'T *WE* STANDING ON THIS LOCATION?
VERY PERCEPTIVE, CAPTAIN.
I LIKE IT. THERE'S HOPE FOR YOU JEDI YET.

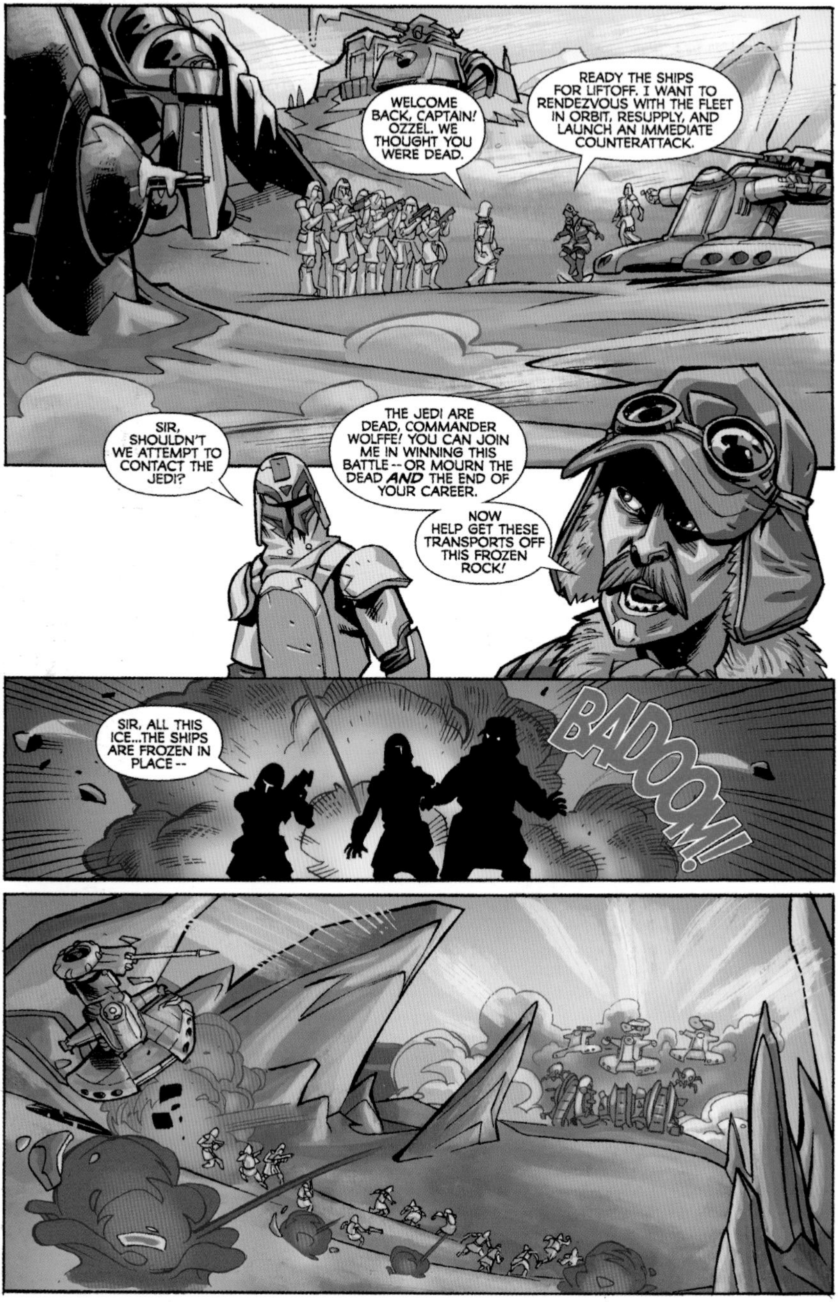
WELCOME BACK, CAPTAIN! OZZEL. WE THOUGHT YOU WERE DEAD.
READY THE SHIPS FOR LIFTOFF. I WANT TO RENDEZVOUS WITH THE FLEET IN ORBIT, RESUPPLY, AND LAUNCH AN IMMEDIATE COUNTERATTACK.
SIR, SHOULDN'T WE ATTEMPT TO CONTACT THE JEDI?
THE JEDI ARE DEAD, COMMANDER WOLFFE! YOU CAN JOIN ME IN WINNING THIS BATTLE -- OR MOURN THE DEAD AND THE END OF YOUR CAREER.
NOW HELP GET THESE TRANSPORTS OFF THIS FROZEN ROCK!
SIR, ALL THIS ICE...THE SHIPS ARE FROZEN IN PLACE --
BADOOM!

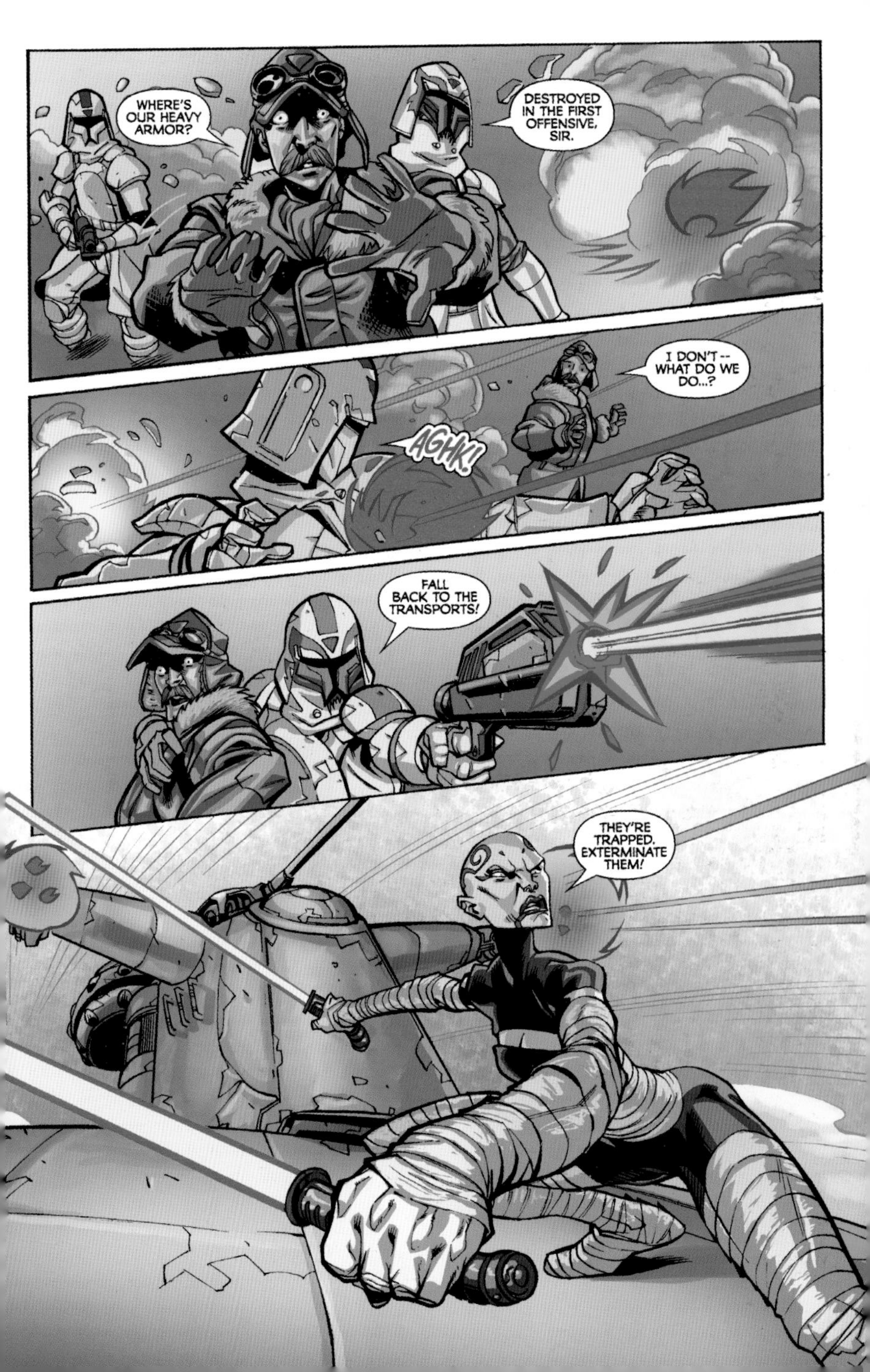
WHERE'S OUR HEAVY ARMOR?
DESTROYED IN THE FIRST OFFENSIVE, SIR.
I DON'T -- WHAT DO WE DO...?
AGHK!
FALL BACK TO THE TRANSPORTS!
THEY'RE TRAPPED. EXTERMINATE THEM!

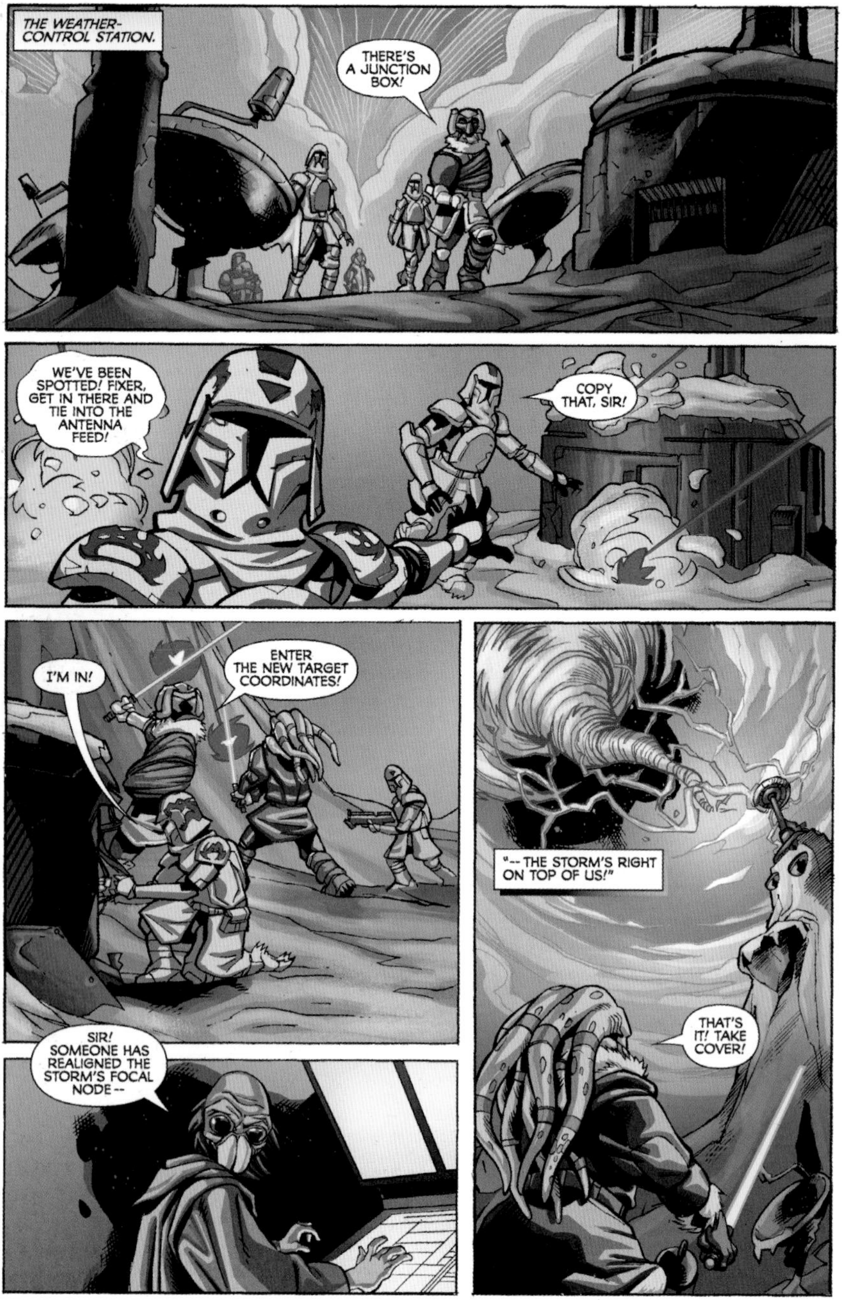
THE WEATHER-CONTROL STATION.
THERE'S A JUNCTION BOX!
WE'VE BEEN SPOTTED! FIXER, GET IN THERE AND TIE INTO THE ANTENNA FEED!
COPY THAT, SIR!
I'M IN!
ENTER THE NEW TARGET COORDINATES!
SIR! SOMEONE HAS REALIGNED THE STORM'S FOCAL NODE --
"-- THE STORM'S RIGHT ON TOP OF US!"
THAT'S IT! TAKE COVER!

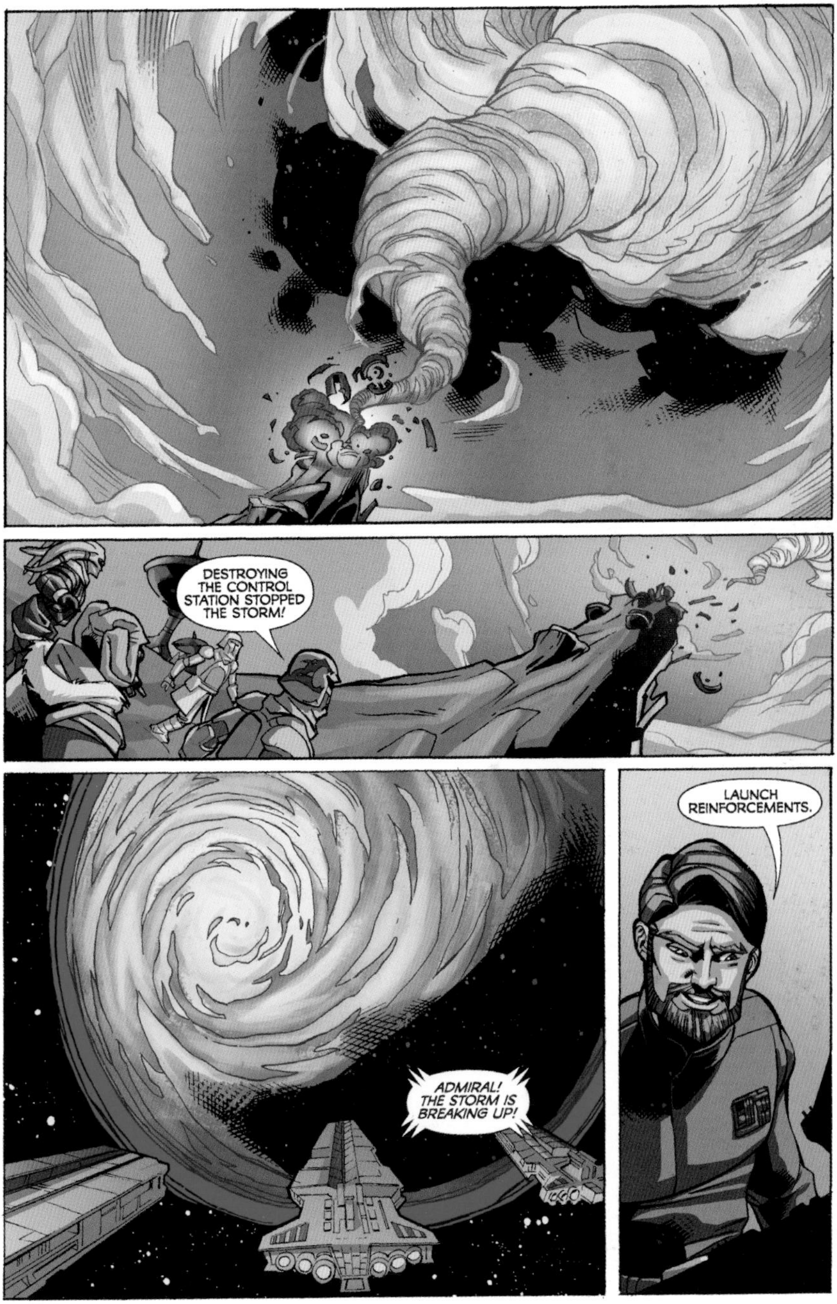
DESTROYING THE CONTROL STATION STOPPED THE STORM!
ADMIRAL! THE STORM IS BREAKING UP!
LAUNCH REINFORCEMENTS.

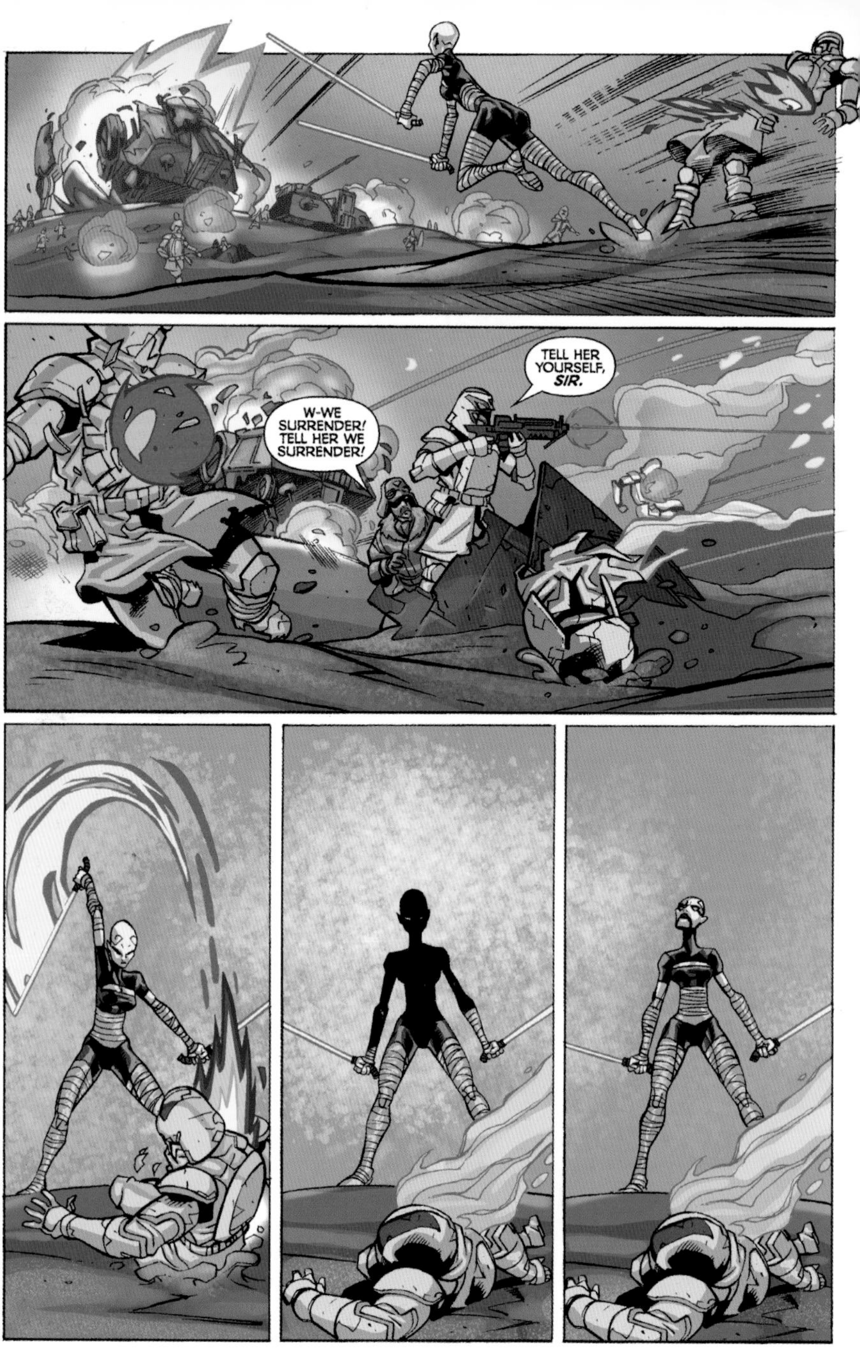
W-WE SURRENDER! TELL HER WE SURRENDER!
TELL HER YOURSELF, SIR.

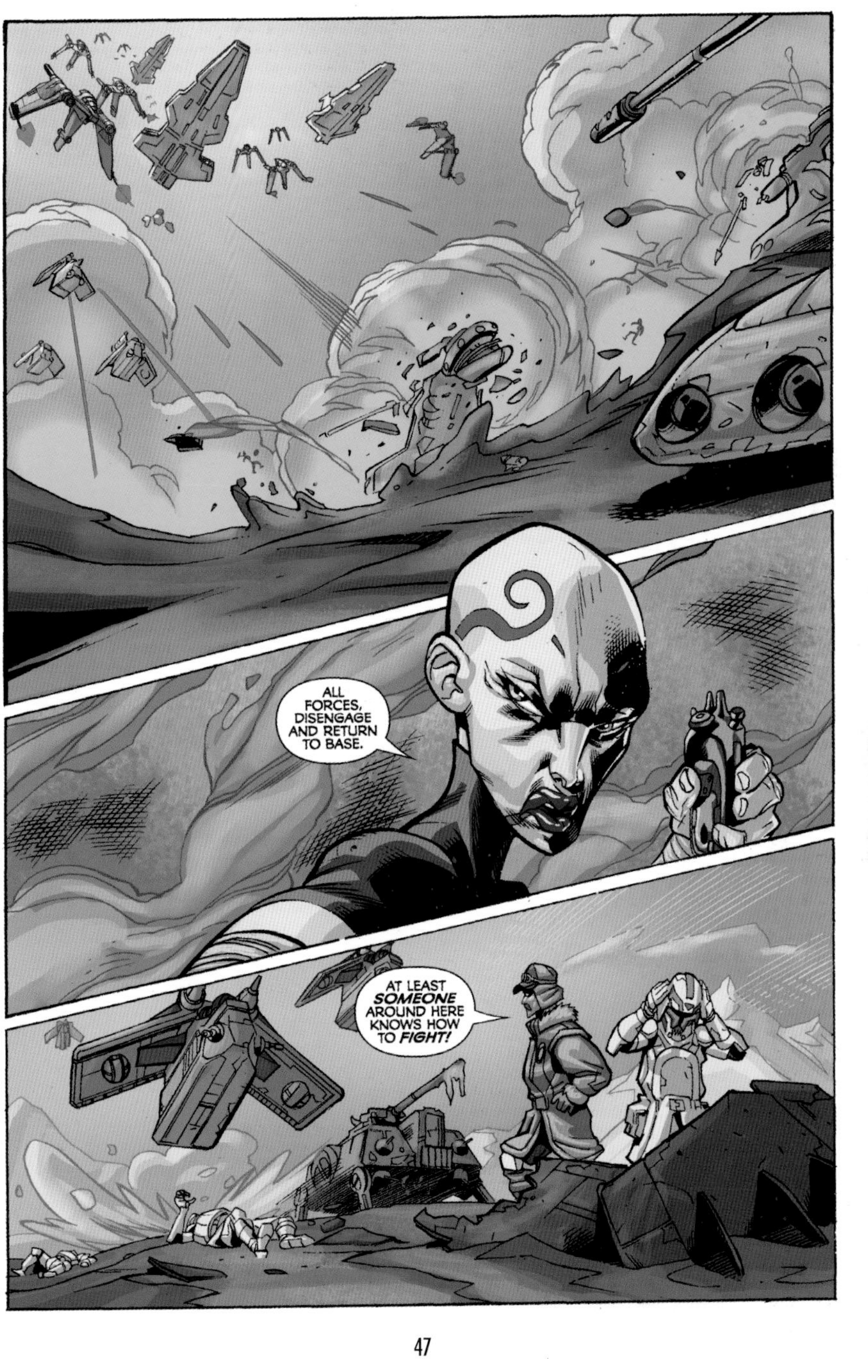
ALL FORCES, DISENGAGE AND RETURN TO BASE.
AT LEAST SOMEONE AROUND HERE KNOWS HOW TO FIGHT!

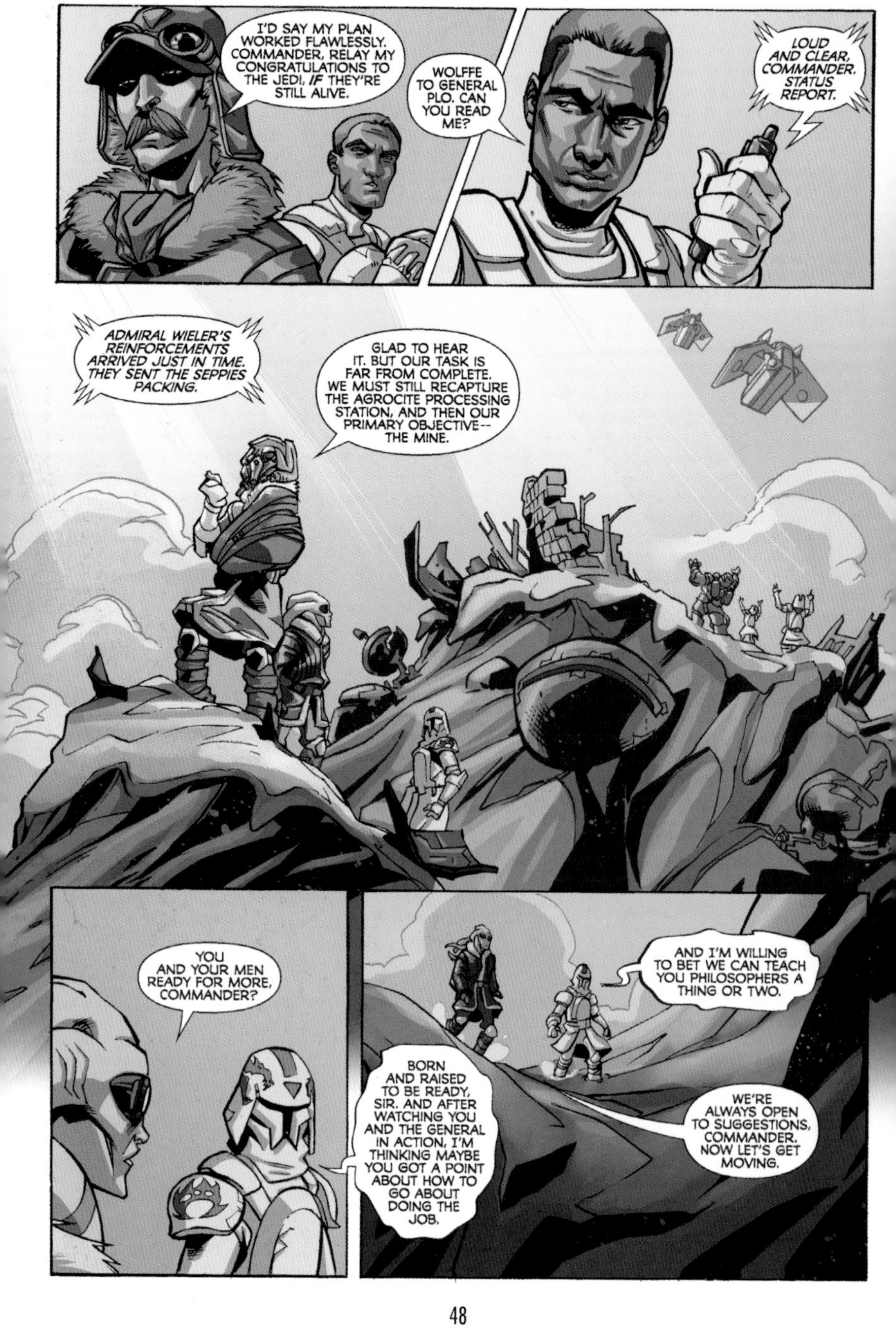
I'D SAY MY PLAN WORKED FLAWLESSLY. COMMANDER, RELAY MY CONGRATULATIONS TO THE JEDI, *IF* THEY'RE STILL ALIVE.
WOLFFE TO GENERAL PLO. CAN YOU READ ME?
LOUD AND CLEAR, COMMANDER. STATUS REPORT.
ADMIRAL WIELER'S REINFORCEMENTS ARRIVED JUST IN TIME. THEY SENT THE SEPPIES PACKING.
GLAD TO HEAR IT. BUT OUR TASK IS FAR FROM COMPLETE. WE MUST STILL RECAPTURE THE AGROCITE PROCESSING STATION, AND THEN OUR PRIMARY OBJECTIVE-- THE MINE.
YOU AND YOUR MEN READY FOR MORE, COMMANDER?
BORN AND RAISED TO BE READY, SIR. AND AFTER WATCHING YOU AND THE GENERAL IN ACTION, I'M THINKING MAYBE YOU GOT A POINT ABOUT HOW TO GO ABOUT DOING THE JOB.
AND I'M WILLING TO BET WE CAN TEACH YOU PHILOSOPHERS A THING OR TWO.
WE'RE ALWAYS OPEN TO SUGGESTIONS, COMMANDER. NOW LET'S GET MOVING.

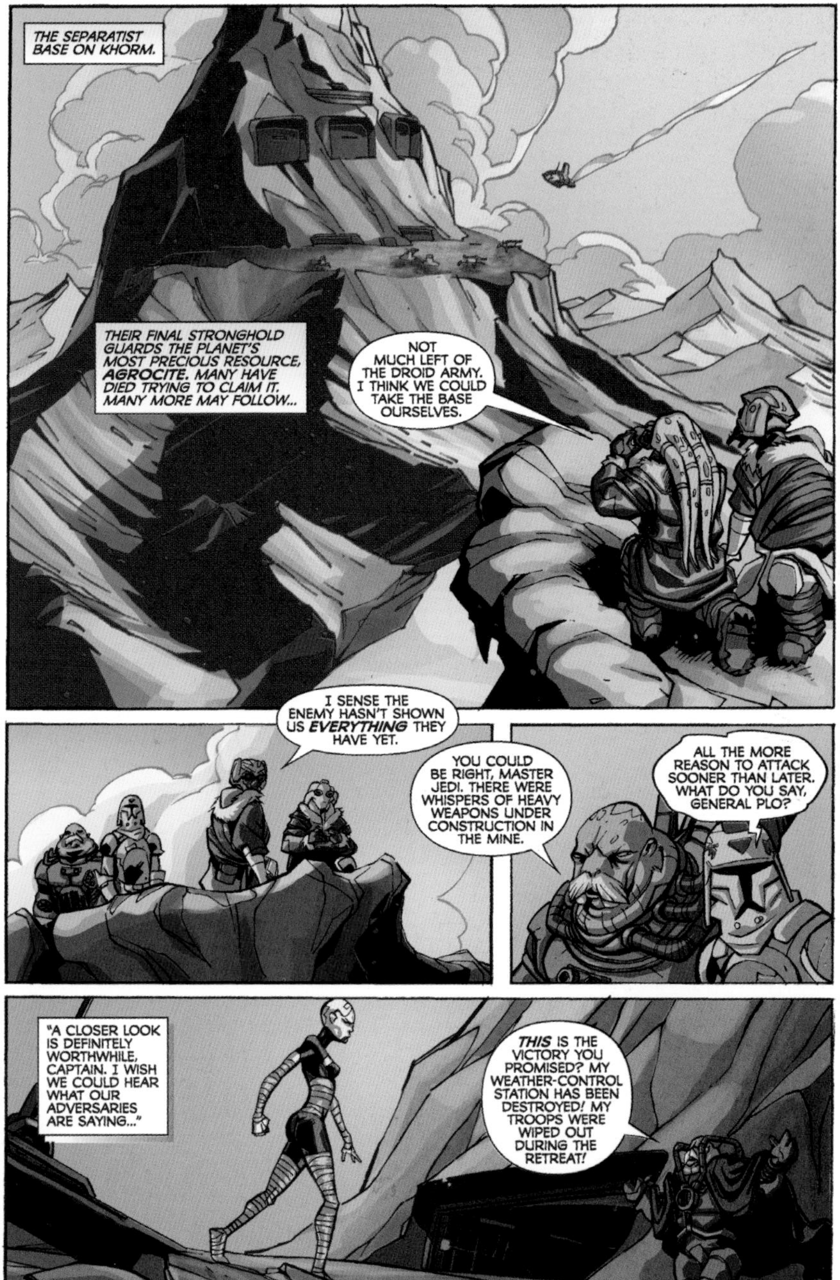
THE SEPARATIST BASE ON KHORM.
THEIR FINAL STRONGHOLD GUARDS THE PLANET'S MOST PRECIOUS RESOURCE, AGROCITE. MANY HAVE DIED TRYING TO CLAIM IT. MANY MORE MAY FOLLOW...
NOT MUCH LEFT OF THE DROID ARMY. I THINK WE COULD TAKE THE BASE OURSELVES.
I SENSE THE ENEMY HASN'T SHOWN US EVERYTHING THEY HAVE YET.
YOU COULD BE RIGHT, MASTER JEDI. THERE WERE WHISPERS OF HEAVY WEAPONS UNDER CONSTRUCTION IN THE MINE.
ALL THE MORE REASON TO ATTACK SOONER THAN LATER. WHAT DO YOU SAY, GENERAL PLO?
"A CLOSER LOOK IS DEFINITELY WORTHWHILE, CAPTAIN. I WISH WE COULD HEAR WHAT OUR ADVERSARIES ARE SAYING..."
THIS IS THE VICTORY YOU PROMISED? MY WEATHER-CONTROL STATION HAS BEEN DESTROYED! MY TROOPS WERE WIPED OUT DURING THE RETREAT!

I SEE *YOU* MANAGED TO SURVIVE.
I HAVE A PLAN TO OVERCOME YOUR FAILURE. MY SLAVES HAVE BEEN MOVED DEEP INTO THE MINES TO BE USED AS HOSTAGES.
ANY PLAN YOU HAVE HAS CEASED TO BE RELEVANT. THE AGROCITE MUST NOT FALL INTO REPUBLIC HANDS.
I ASSURE YOU, ASSASSIN, MY DEFENSES HERE ARE IMPENETRABLE. WE CAN HOLD THIS POSITION INDEFINITELY.
IF YOU CAN HOLD OUT FOR EVEN *ONE* PLANETARY ROTATION, I'LL BE PLEASANTLY SURPRISED.
RIG THE MINES WITH THERMAL CHARGES. KEY THEM TO THIS DETONATOR.
YES, MISTRESS.
THAT'S NOT PART OF MY PLAN!
LOOKS LIKE THEY'RE MOVING EXPLOSIVES INTO THE MINE.

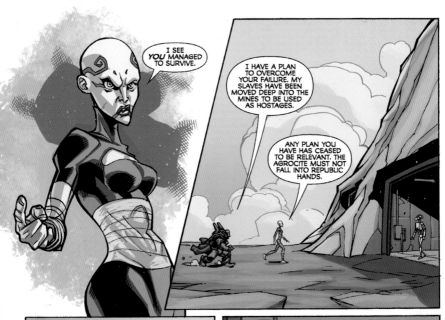

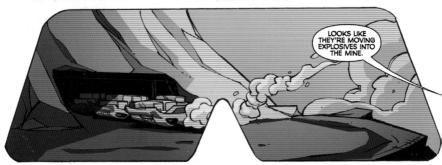

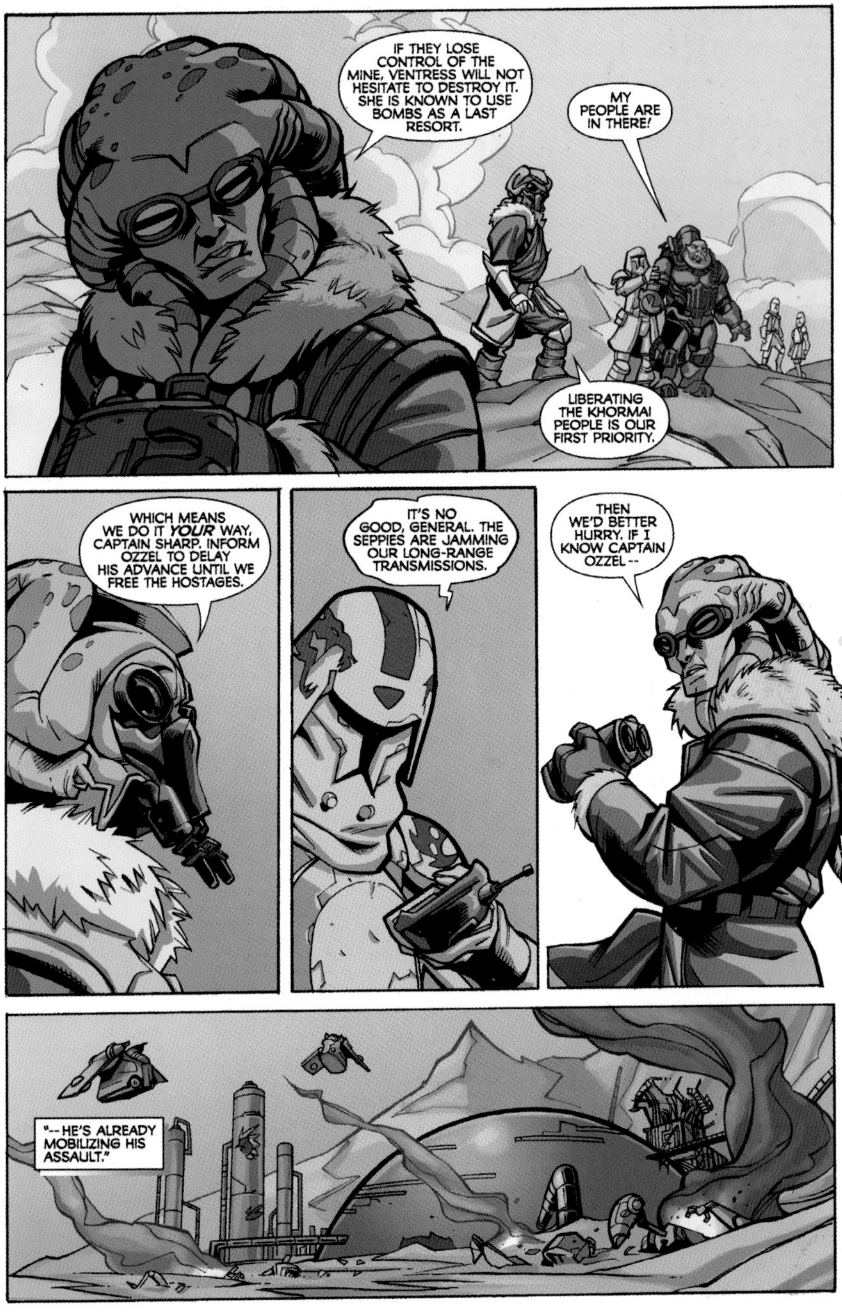
IF THEY LOSE CONTROL OF THE MINE, VENTRESS WILL NOT HESITATE TO DESTROY IT. SHE IS KNOWN TO USE BOMBS AS A LAST RESORT.
MY PEOPLE ARE IN THERE!
LIBERATING THE KHORMAI PEOPLE IS OUR FIRST PRIORITY.
WHICH MEANS WE DO IT YOUR WAY, CAPTAIN SHARP. INFORM OZZEL TO DELAY HIS ADVANCE UNTIL WE FREE THE HOSTAGES.
IT'S NO GOOD, GENERAL. THE SEPPIES ARE JAMMING OUR LONG-RANGE TRANSMISSIONS.
THEN WE'D BETTER HURRY. IF I KNOW CAPTAIN OZZEL --
"-- HE'S ALREADY MOBILIZING HIS ASSAULT."

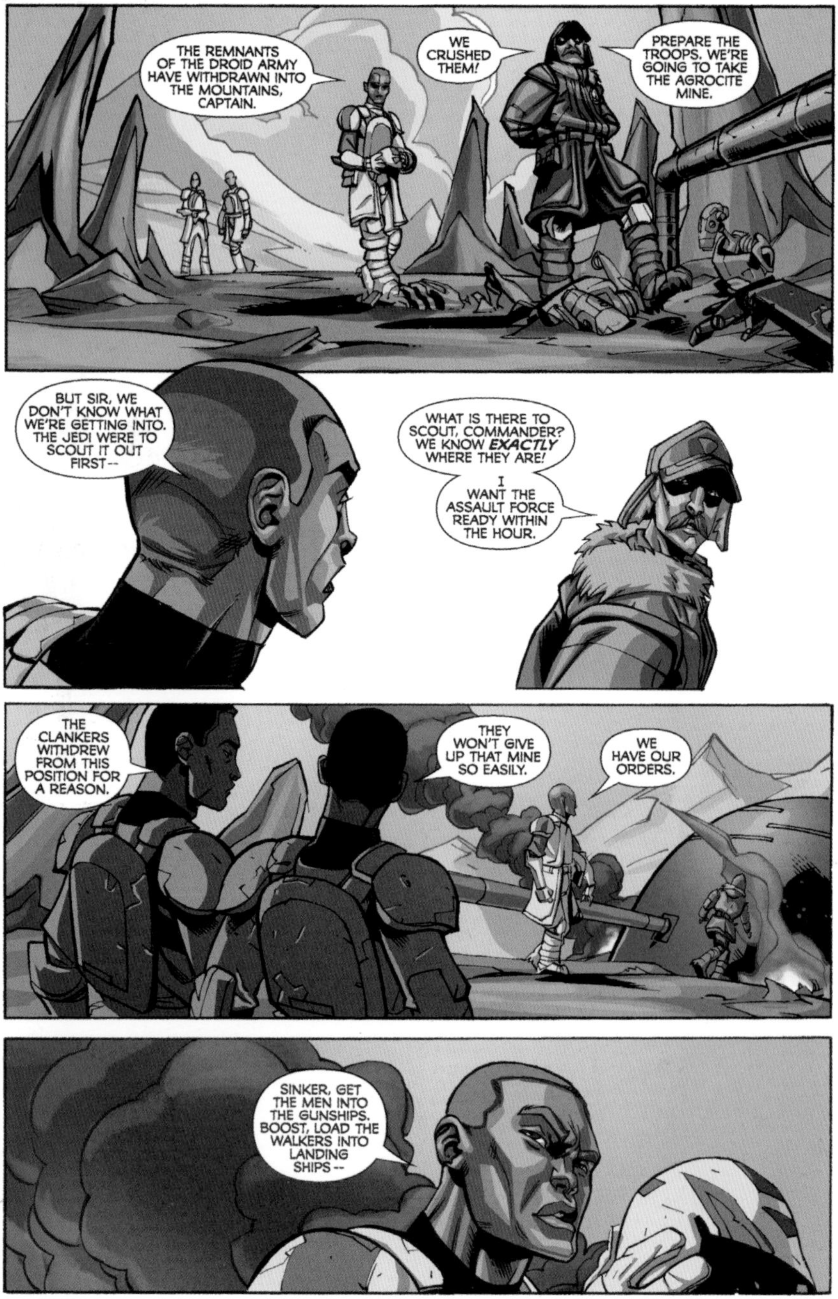
THE REMNANTS OF THE DROID ARMY HAVE WITHDRAWN INTO THE MOUNTAINS, CAPTAIN.
WE CRUSHED THEM!
PREPARE THE TROOPS. WE'RE GOING TO TAKE THE AGROCITE MINE.
BUT SIR, WE DON'T KNOW WHAT WE'RE GETTING INTO. THE JEDI WERE TO SCOUT IT OUT FIRST--
WHAT IS THERE TO SCOUT, COMMANDER? WE KNOW *EXACTLY* WHERE THEY ARE!
I WANT THE ASSAULT FORCE READY WITHIN THE HOUR.
THE CLANKERS WITHDREW FROM THIS POSITION FOR A REASON.
THEY WON'T GIVE UP THAT MINE SO EASILY.
WE HAVE OUR ORDERS.
SINKER, GET THE MEN INTO THE GUNSHIPS. BOOST, LOAD THE WALKERS INTO LANDING SHIPS --

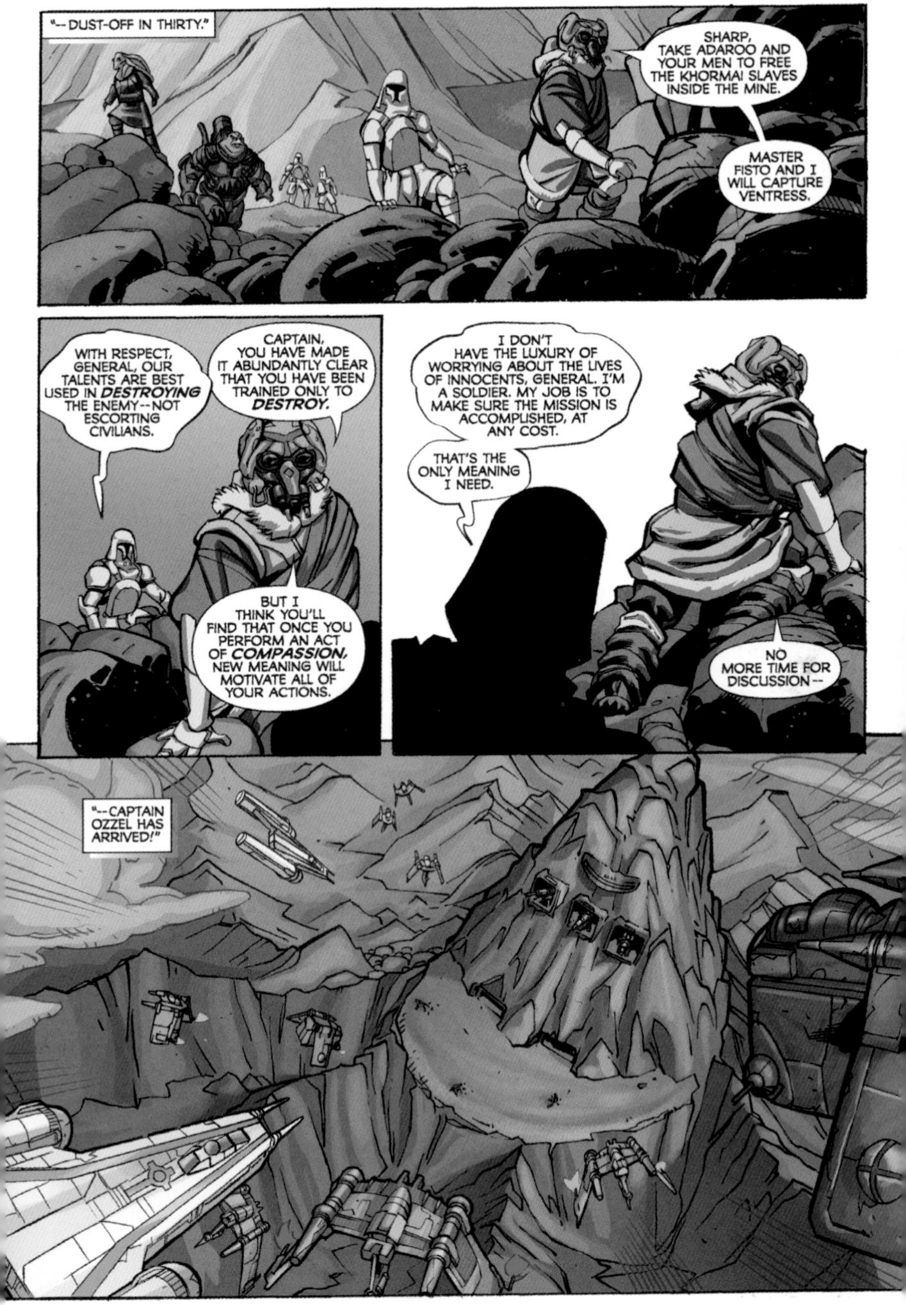
"--DUST-OFF IN THIRTY."
SHARP, TAKE ADAROO AND YOUR MEN TO FREE THE KHORMAI SLAVES INSIDE THE MINE.
MASTER FISTO AND I WILL CAPTURE VENTRESS.
WITH RESPECT, GENERAL, OUR TALENTS ARE BEST USED IN DESTROYING THE ENEMY--NOT ESCORTING CIVILIANS.
CAPTAIN, YOU HAVE MADE IT ABUNDANTLY CLEAR THAT YOU HAVE BEEN TRAINED ONLY TO DESTROY.
BUT I THINK YOU'LL FIND THAT ONCE YOU PERFORM AN ACT OF COMPASSION, NEW MEANING WILL MOTIVATE ALL OF YOUR ACTIONS.
I DON'T HAVE THE LUXURY OF WORRYING ABOUT THE LIVES OF INNOCENTS, GENERAL. I'M A SOLDIER. MY JOB IS TO MAKE SURE THE MISSION IS ACCOMPLISHED, AT ANY COST.
THAT'S THE ONLY MEANING I NEED.
NO MORE TIME FOR DISCUSSION--
"--CAPTAIN OZZEL HAS ARRIVED!"

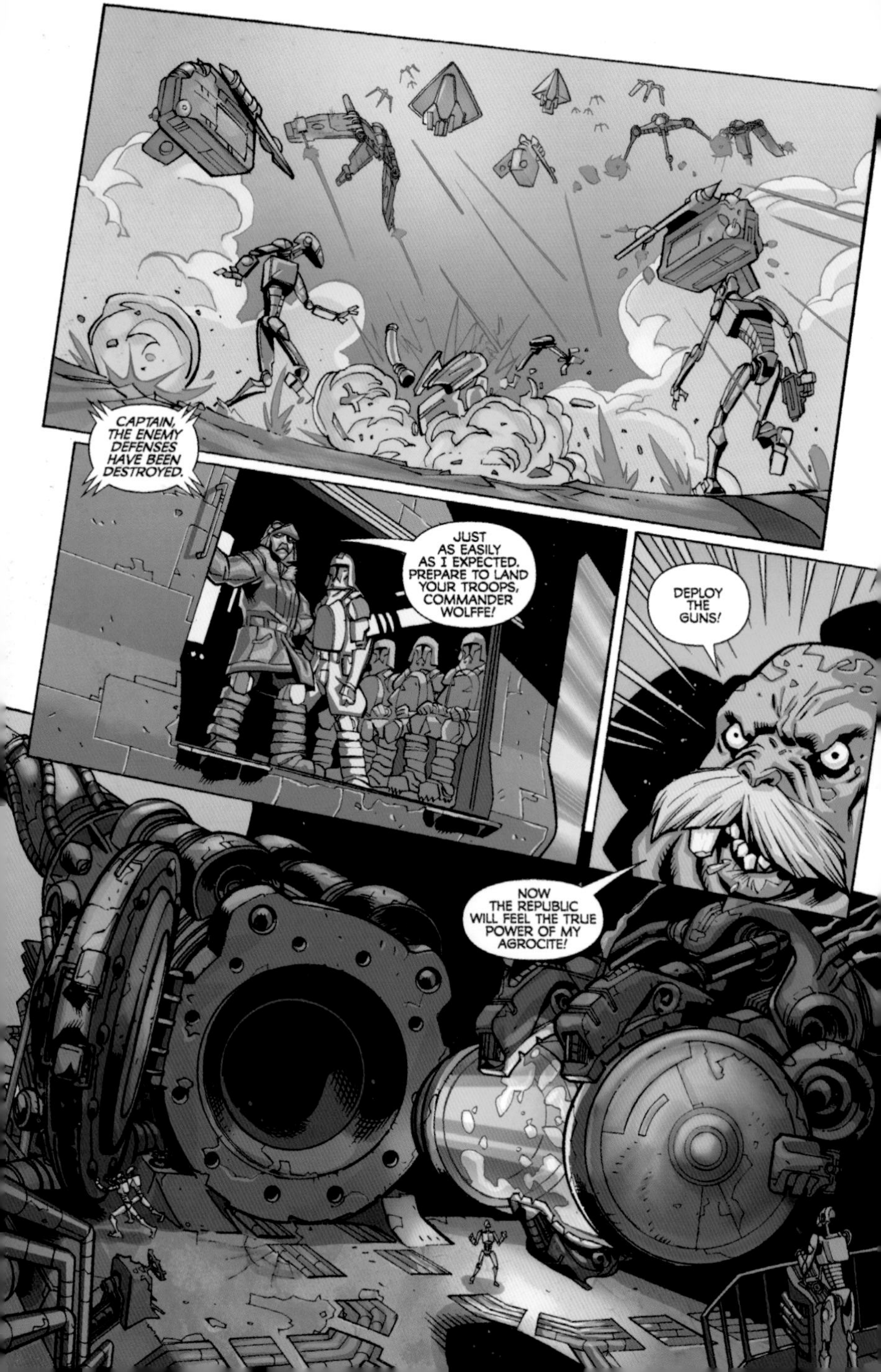
CAPTAIN, THE ENEMY DEFENSES HAVE BEEN DESTROYED.
JUST AS EASILY AS I EXPECTED. PREPARE TO LAND YOUR TROOPS, COMMANDER WOLFFE!
DEPLOY THE GUNS!
NOW THE REPUBLIC WILL FEEL THE TRUE POWER OF MY AGROCITE!

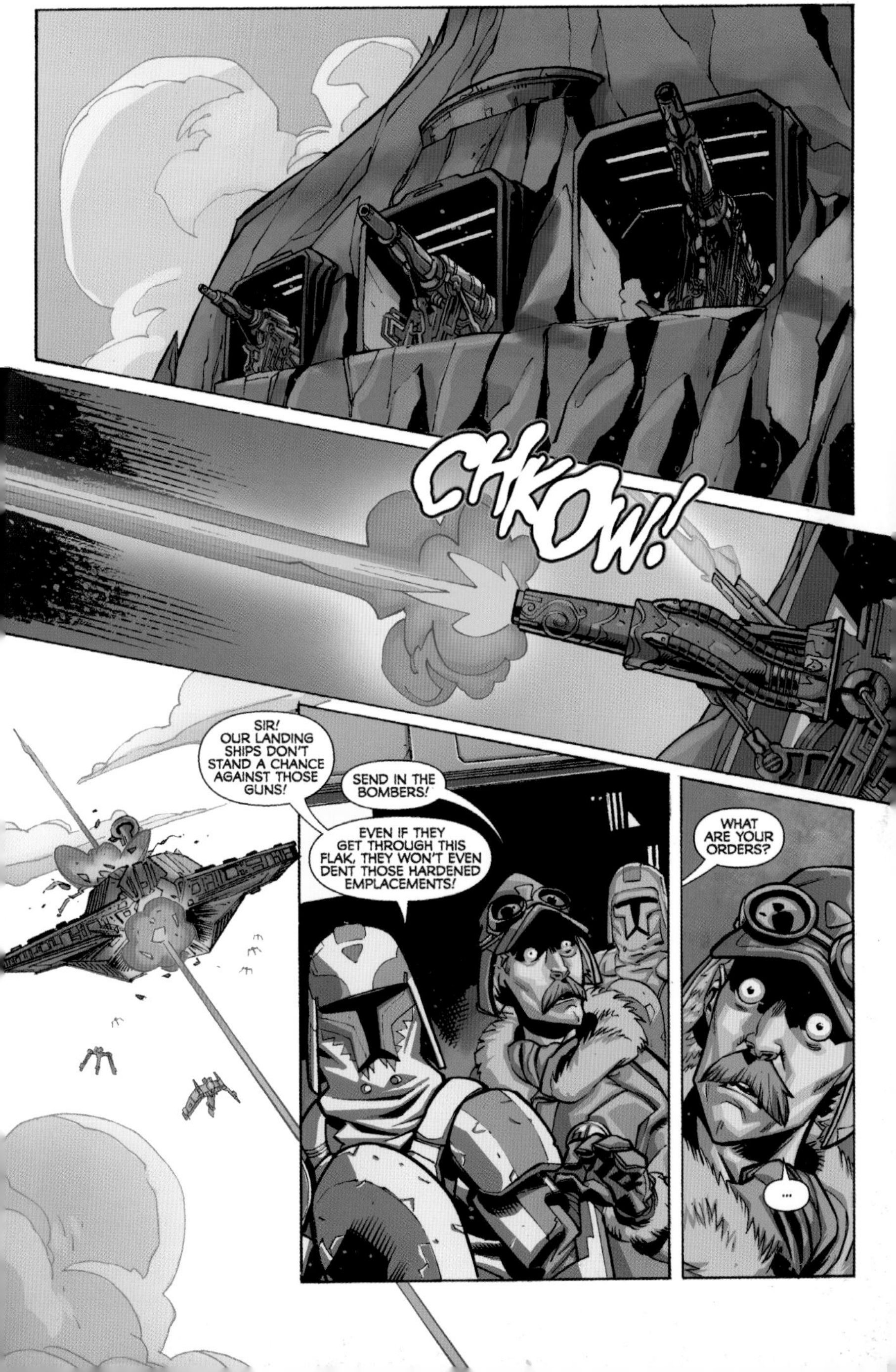
CHKOW!
SIR! OUR LANDING SHIPS DON'T STAND A CHANCE AGAINST THOSE GUNS!
SEND IN THE BOMBERS!
EVEN IF THEY GET THROUGH THIS FLAK, THEY WON'T EVEN DENT THOSE HARDENED EMPLACEMENTS!
WHAT ARE YOUR ORDERS?
...

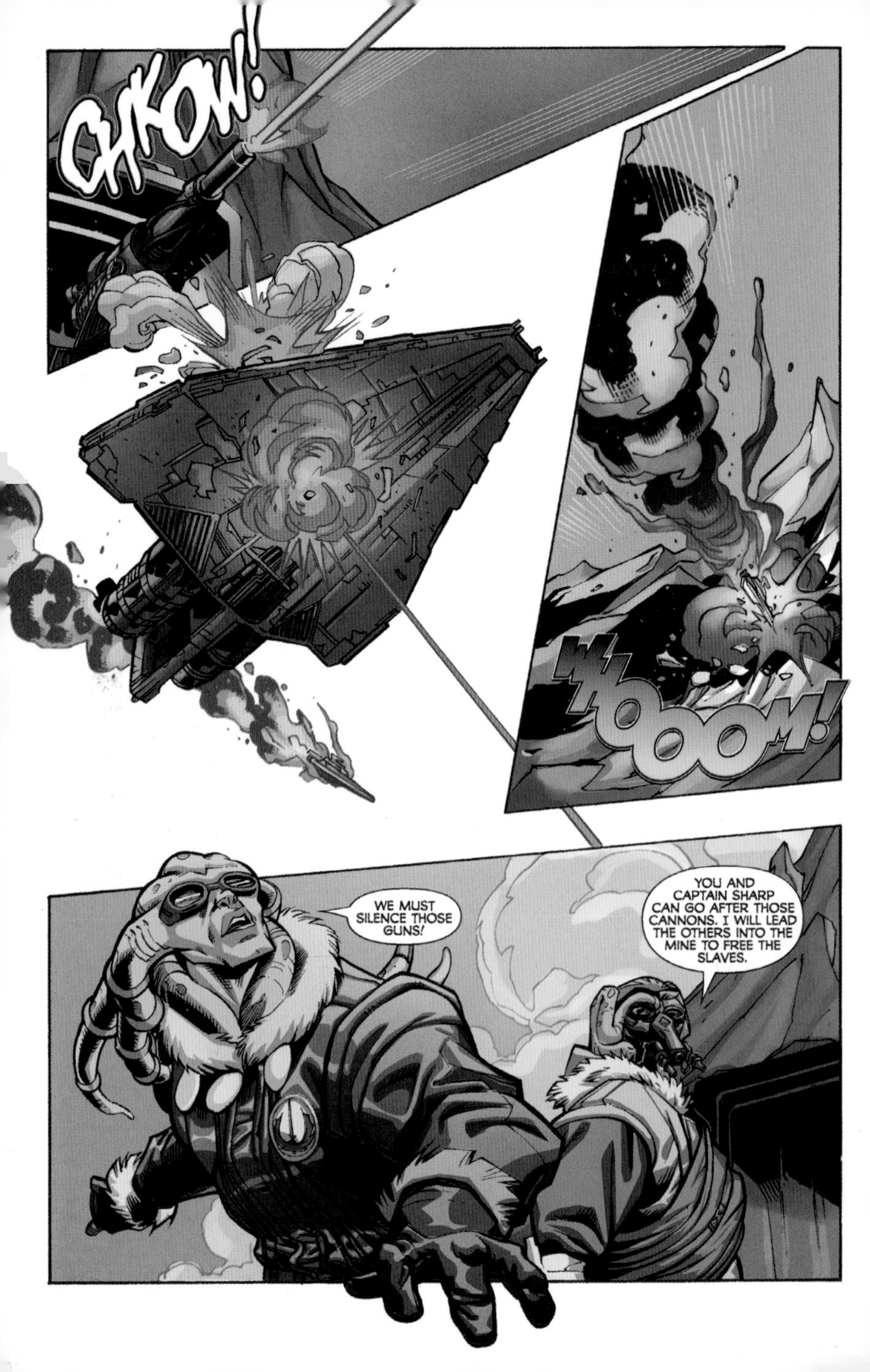
CHKOW!
WHOOOOM!
WE MUST SILENCE THOSE GUNS!
YOU AND CAPTAIN SHARP CAN GO AFTER THOSE CANNONS. I WILL LEAD THE OTHERS INTO THE MINE TO FREE THE SLAVES.

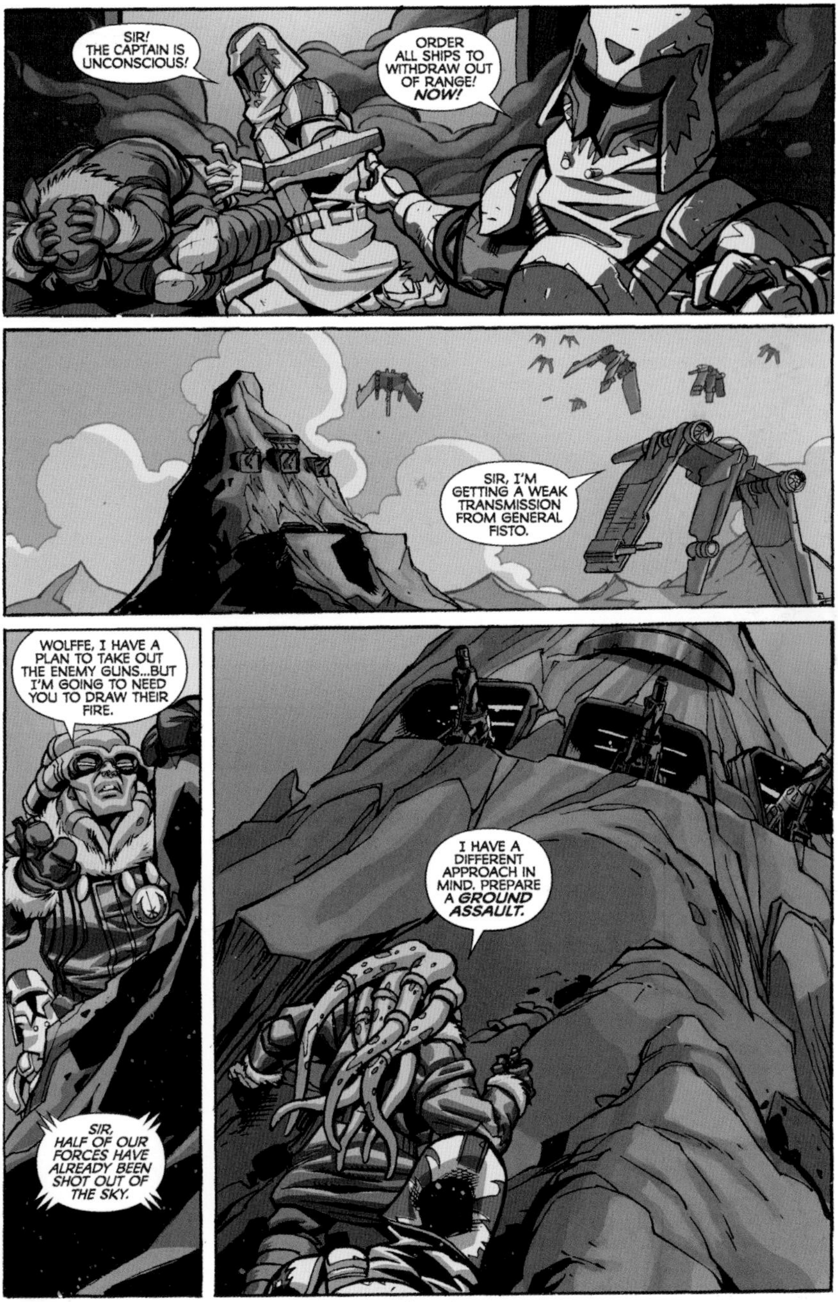
SIR! THE CAPTAIN IS UNCONSCIOUS!
ORDER ALL SHIPS TO WITHDRAW OUT OF RANGE! *NOW!*
SIR, I'M GETTING A WEAK TRANSMISSION FROM GENERAL FISTO.
WOLFFE, I HAVE A PLAN TO TAKE OUT THE ENEMY GUNS...BUT I'M GOING TO NEED YOU TO DRAW THEIR FIRE.
SIR, HALF OF OUR FORCES HAVE ALREADY BEEN SHOT OUT OF THE SKY.
I HAVE A DIFFERENT APPROACH IN MIND. PREPARE A ***GROUND ASSAULT.***

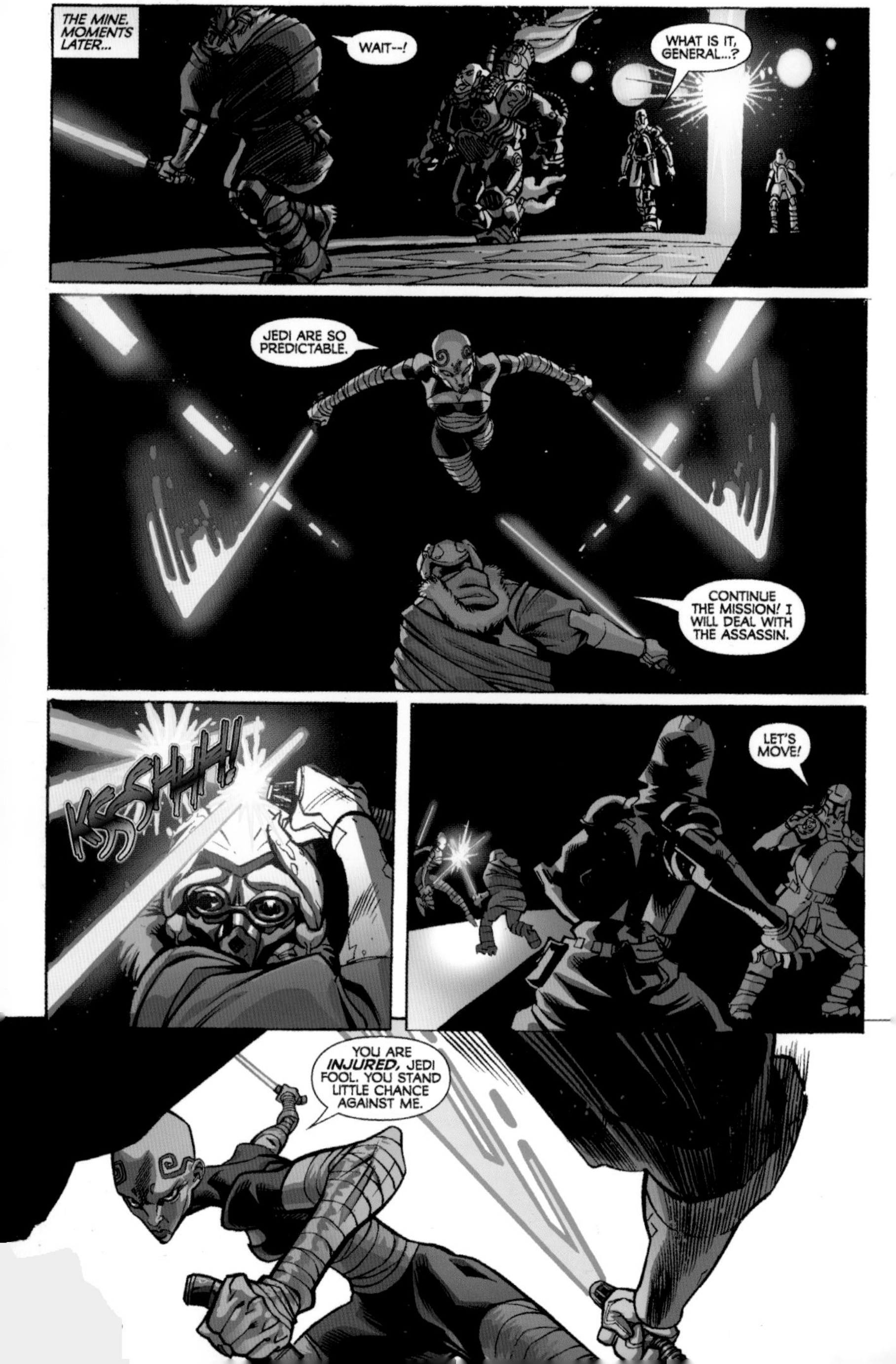
THE MINE. MOMENTS LATER...
WAIT--!
WHAT IS IT, GENERAL...?
JEDI ARE SO PREDICTABLE.
CONTINUE THE MISSION! I WILL DEAL WITH THE ASSASSIN.
KSSHHH!
LET'S MOVE!
YOU ARE INJURED, JEDI FOOL. YOU STAND LITTLE CHANCE AGAINST ME.

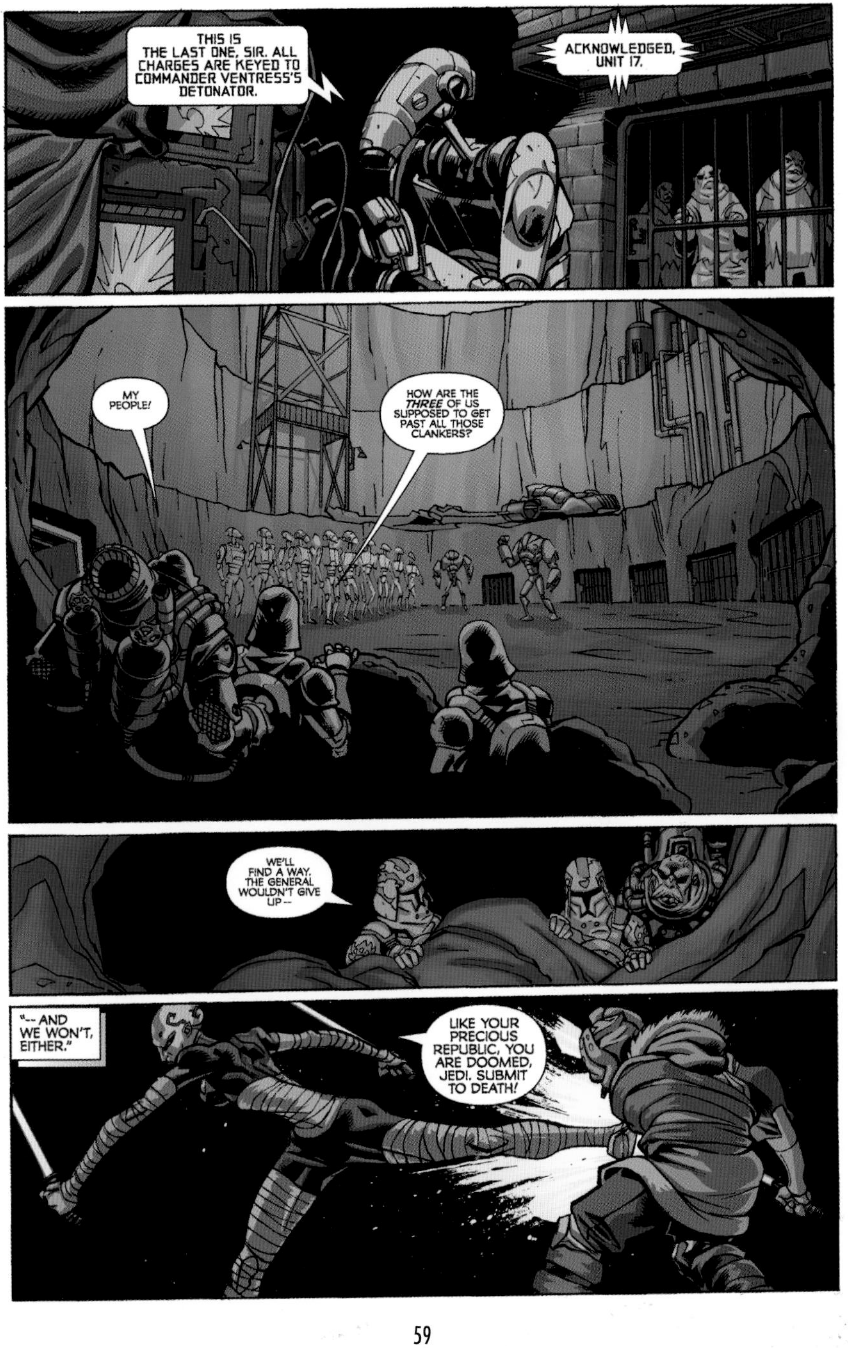
THIS IS THE LAST ONE, SIR. ALL CHARGES ARE KEYED TO COMMANDER VENTRESS'S DETONATOR.
ACKNOWLEDGED, UNIT 17.
MY PEOPLE!
HOW ARE THE *THREE* OF US SUPPOSED TO GET PAST ALL THOSE CLANKERS?
WE'LL FIND A WAY. THE GENERAL WOULDN'T GIVE UP--
"-- AND WE WON'T, EITHER."
LIKE YOUR PRECIOUS REPUBLIC, YOU ARE DOOMED, JEDI. SUBMIT TO DEATH!

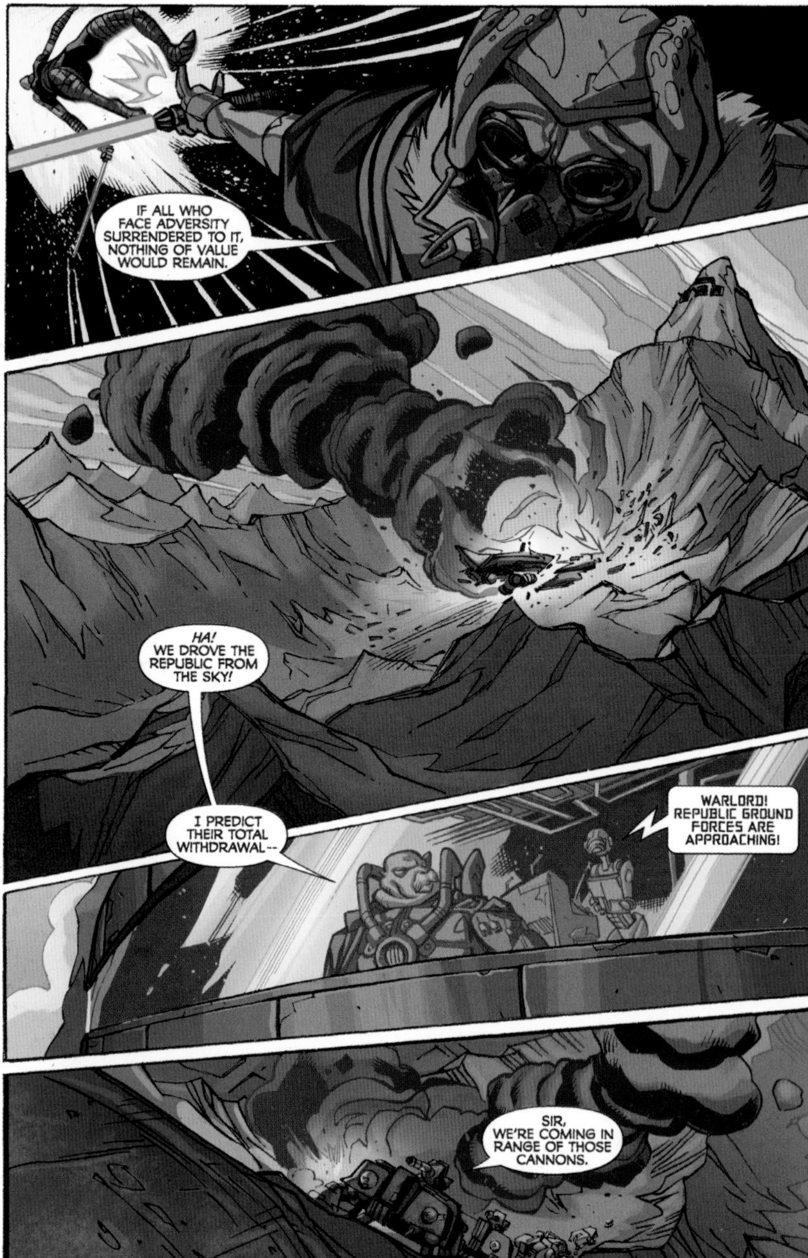
IF ALL WHO FACE ADVERSITY SURRENDERED TO IT, NOTHING OF VALUE WOULD REMAIN.
HA! WE DROVE THE REPUBLIC FROM THE SKY!
I PREDICT THEIR TOTAL WITHDRAWAL--
WARLORD! REPUBLIC GROUND FORCES ARE APPROACHING!
SIR, WE'RE COMING IN RANGE OF THOSE CANNONS.

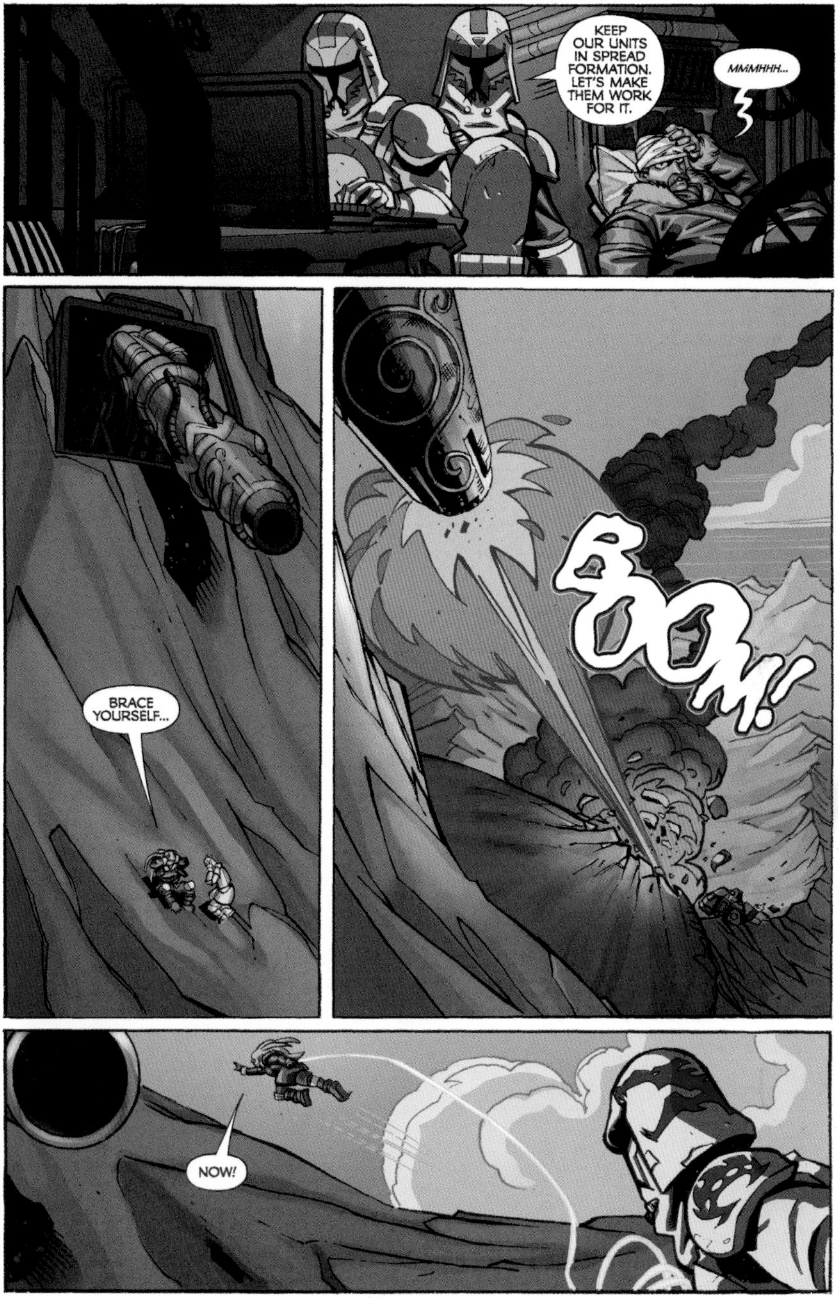
KEEP OUR UNITS IN SPREAD FORMATION. LET'S MAKE THEM WORK FOR IT.
MMMHHH...
BRACE YOURSELF...
BOOM!!
NOW!

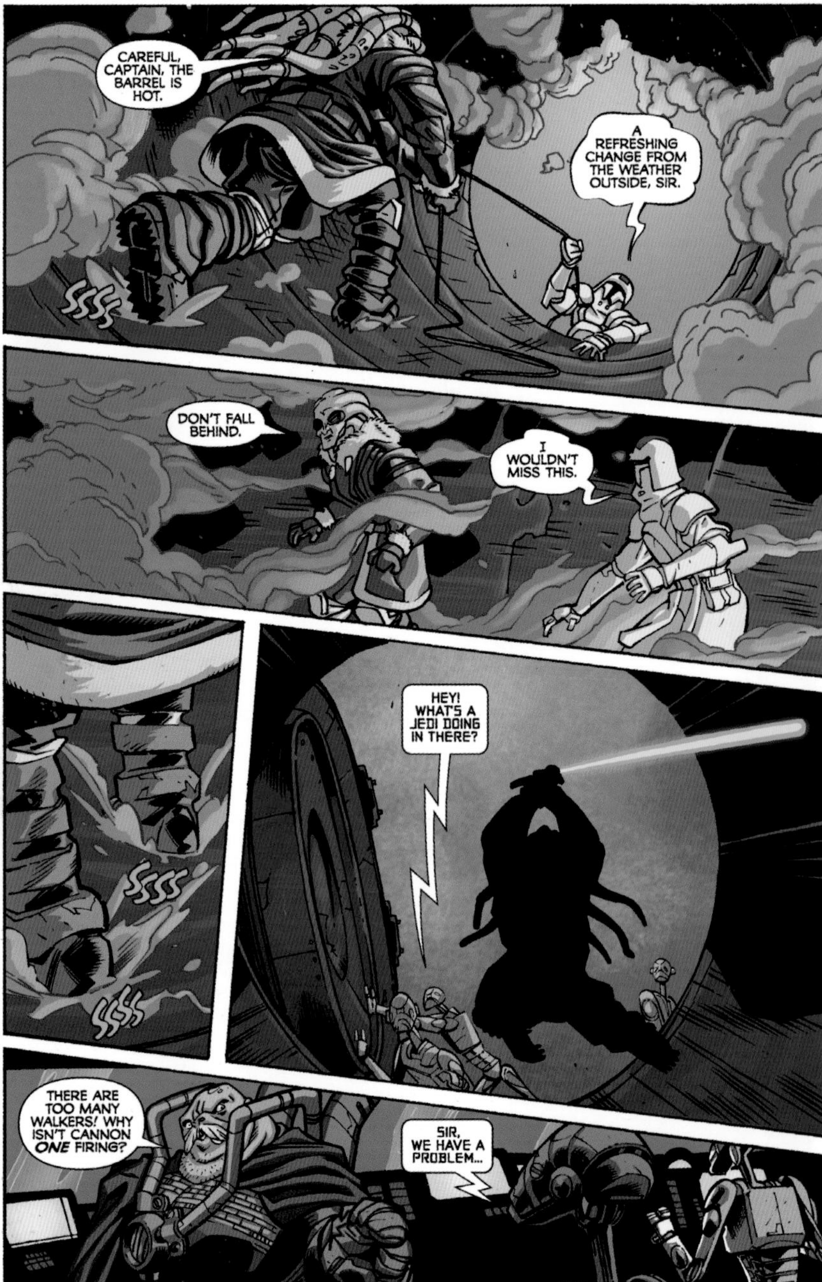
CAREFUL, CAPTAIN, THE BARREL IS HOT.
A REFRESHING CHANGE FROM THE WEATHER OUTSIDE, SIR.
SSSS
DON'T FALL BEHIND.
I WOULDN'T MISS THIS.
SSSS
SSSS
HEY! WHAT'S A JEDI DOING IN THERE?
THERE ARE TOO MANY WALKERS! WHY ISN'T CANNON *ONE* FIRING?
SIR, WE HAVE A PROBLEM...

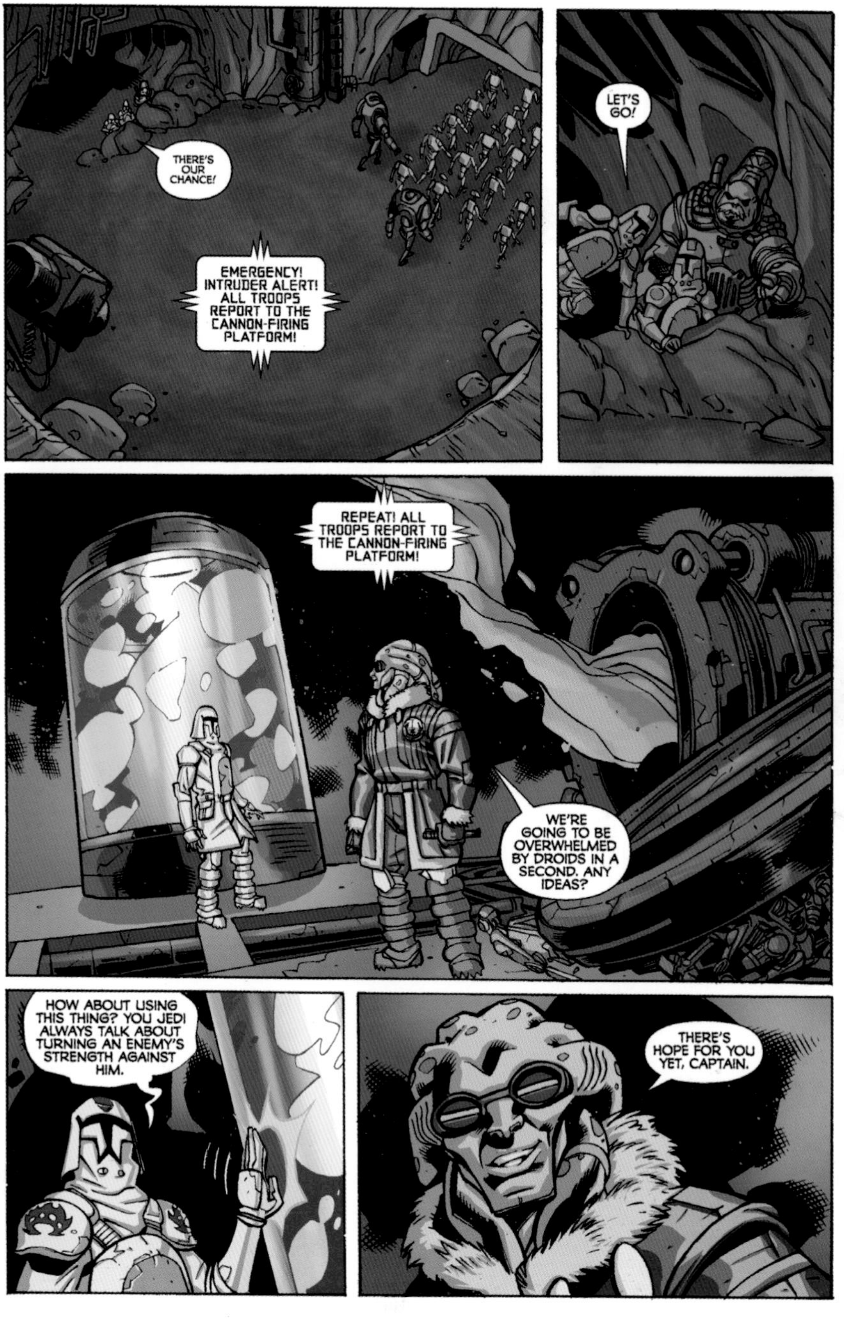
THERE'S OUR CHANCE!
EMERGENCY! INTRUDER ALERT! ALL TROOPS REPORT TO THE CANNON-FIRING PLATFORM!
LET'S GO!
REPEAT! ALL TROOPS REPORT TO THE CANNON-FIRING PLATFORM!
WE'RE GOING TO BE OVERWHELMED BY DROIDS IN A SECOND. ANY IDEAS?
HOW ABOUT USING THIS THING? YOU JEDI ALWAYS TALK ABOUT TURNING AN ENEMY'S STRENGTH AGAINST HIM.
THERE'S HOPE FOR YOU YET, CAPTAIN.

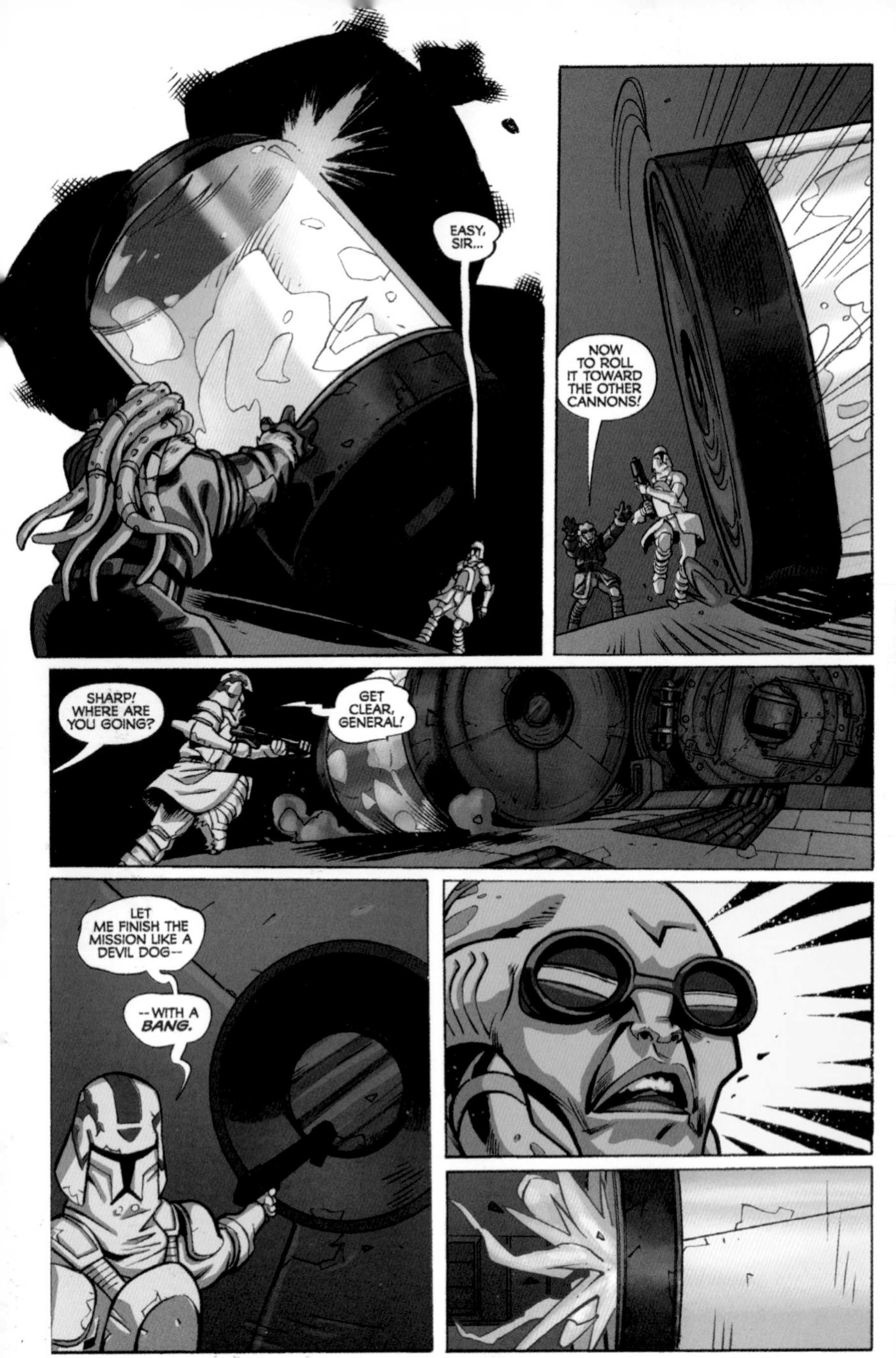
EASY, SIR...
NOW TO ROLL IT TOWARD THE OTHER CANNONS!
SHARP! WHERE ARE YOU GOING?
GET CLEAR, GENERAL!
LET ME FINISH THE MISSION LIKE A DEVIL DOG--
--WITH A *BANG.*

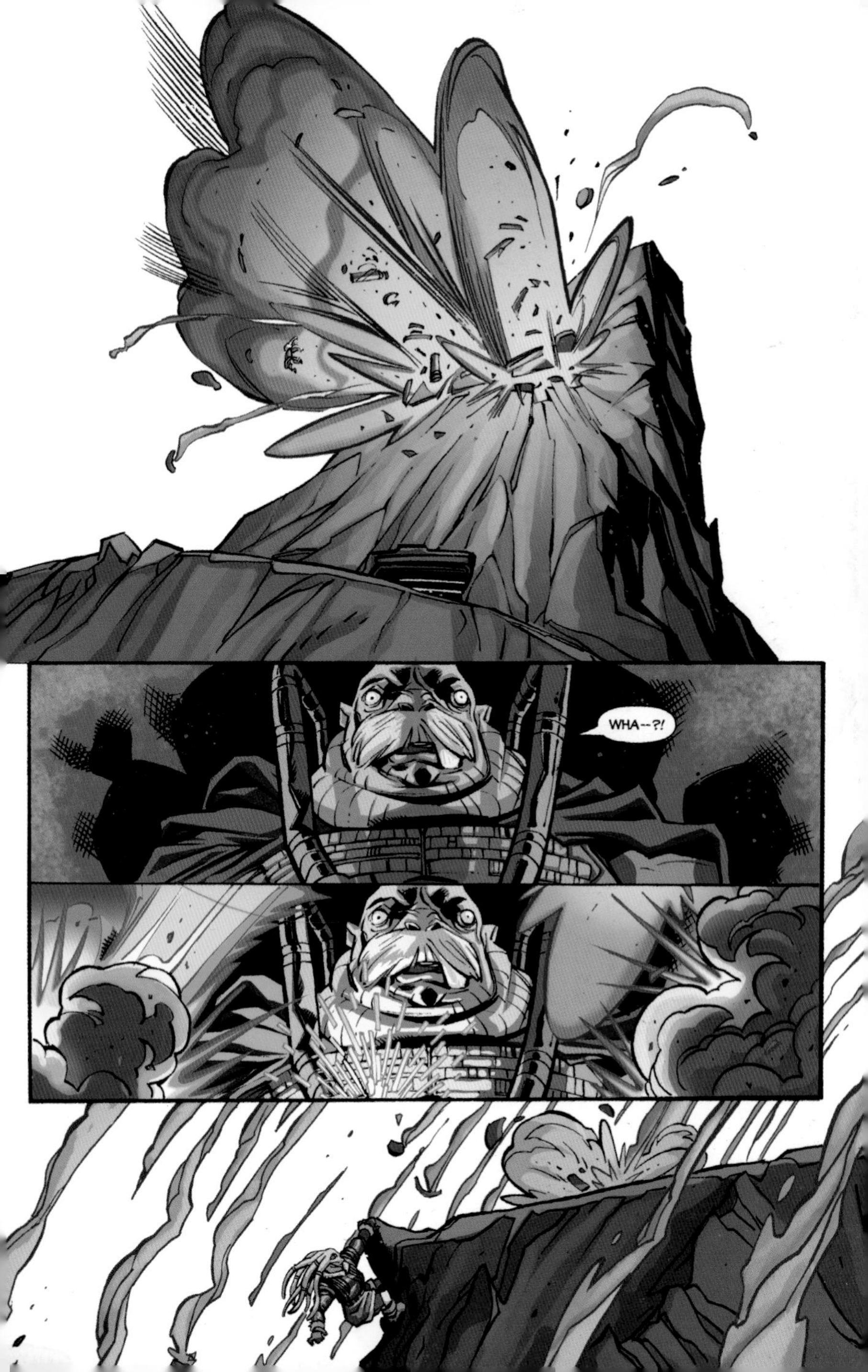
WHA--?!

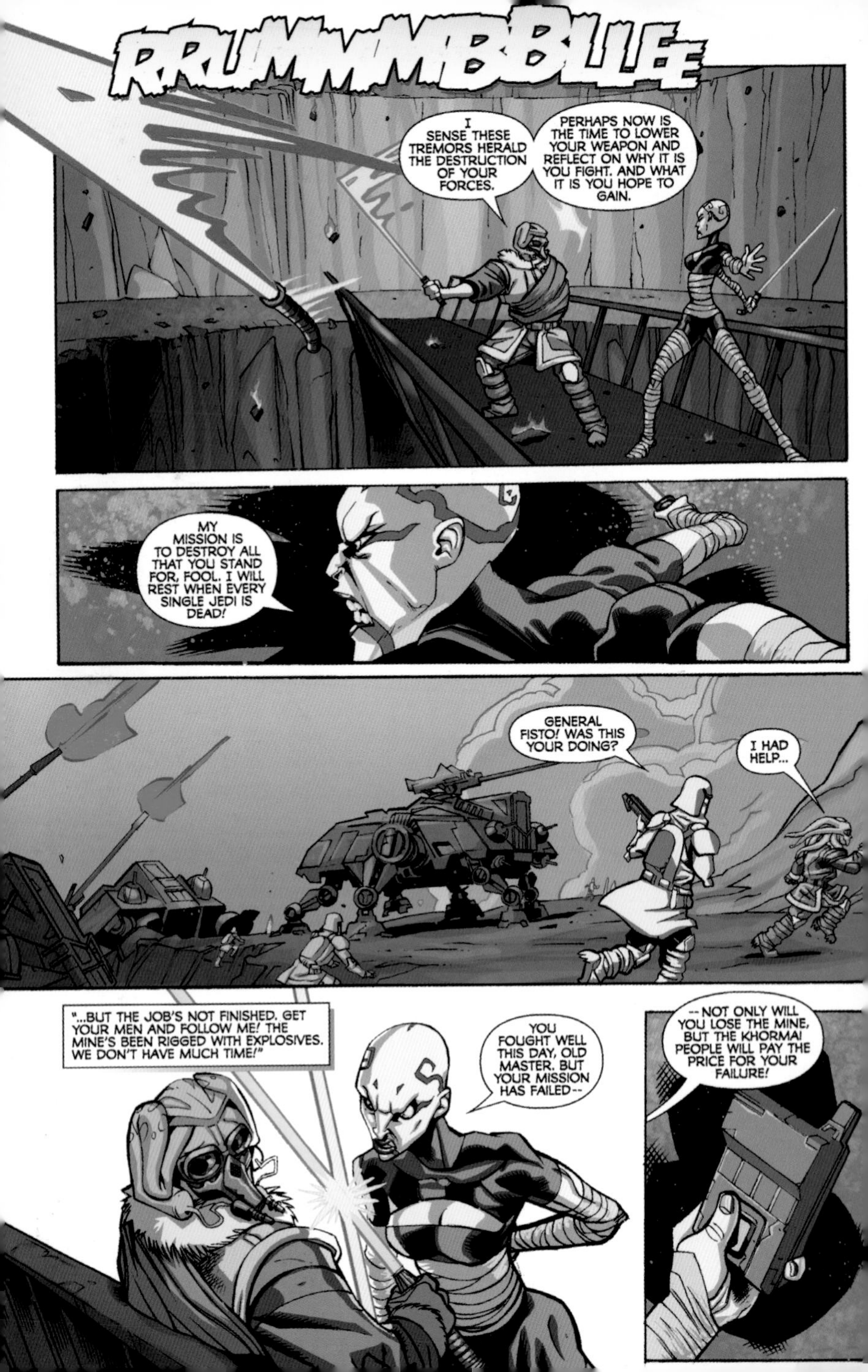
RRUMMMBBLLEE
I SENSE THESE TREMORS HERALD THE DESTRUCTION OF YOUR FORCES.
PERHAPS NOW IS THE TIME TO LOWER YOUR WEAPON AND REFLECT ON WHY IT IS YOU FIGHT. AND WHAT IT IS YOU HOPE TO GAIN.
MY MISSION IS TO DESTROY ALL THAT YOU STAND FOR, FOOL. I WILL REST WHEN EVERY SINGLE JEDI IS DEAD!
GENERAL FISTO! WAS THIS YOUR DOING?
I HAD HELP...
"...BUT THE JOB'S NOT FINISHED. GET YOUR MEN AND FOLLOW ME! THE MINE'S BEEN RIGGED WITH EXPLOSIVES. WE DON'T HAVE MUCH TIME!"
YOU FOUGHT WELL THIS DAY, OLD MASTER. BUT YOUR MISSION HAS FAILED--
--NOT ONLY WILL YOU LOSE THE MINE, BUT THE KHORMAI PEOPLE WILL PAY THE PRICE FOR YOUR FAILURE!

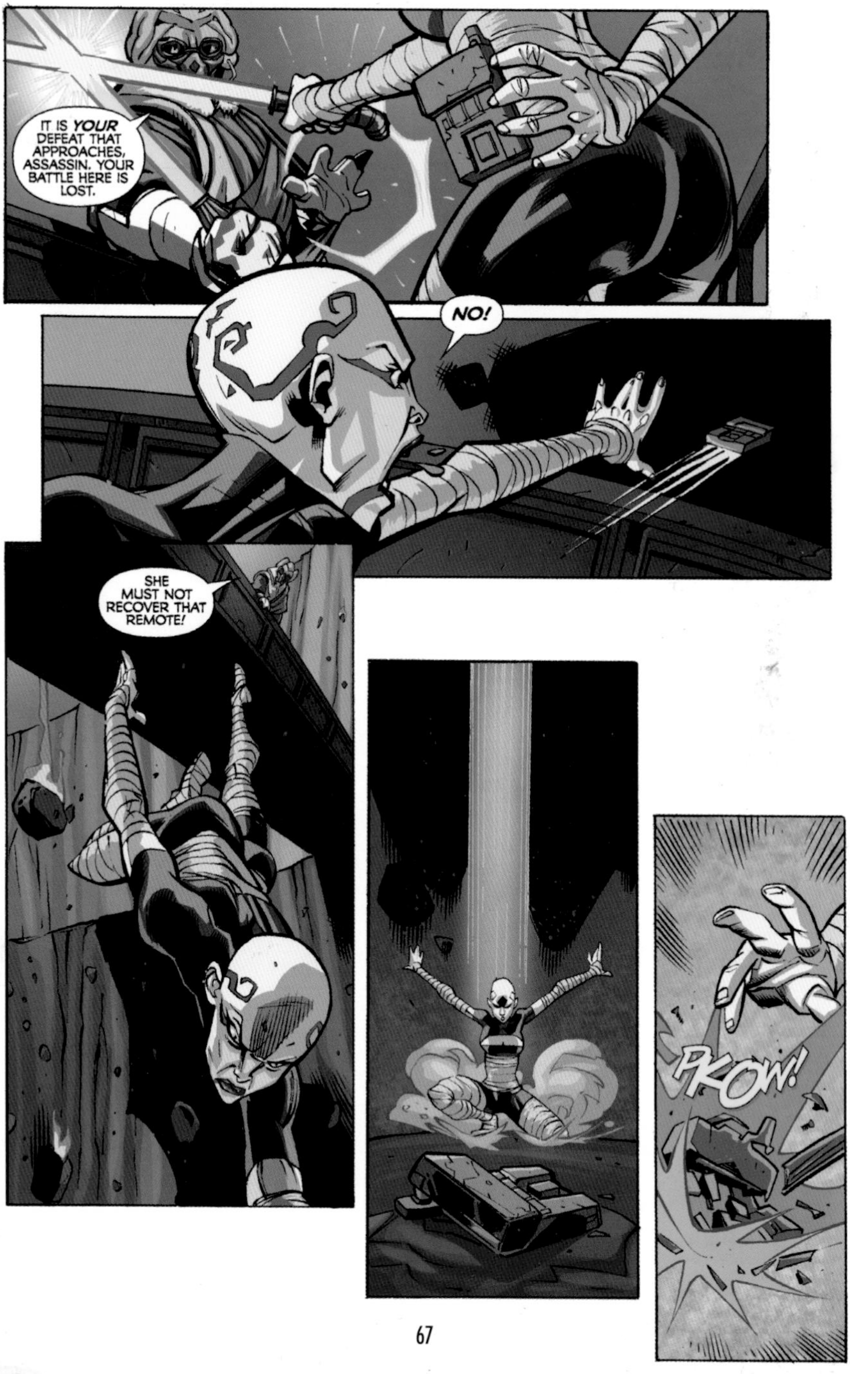
IT IS *YOUR* DEFEAT THAT APPROACHES, ASSASSIN. YOUR BATTLE HERE IS LOST.
NO!
SHE MUST NOT RECOVER THAT REMOTE!
PKOW!

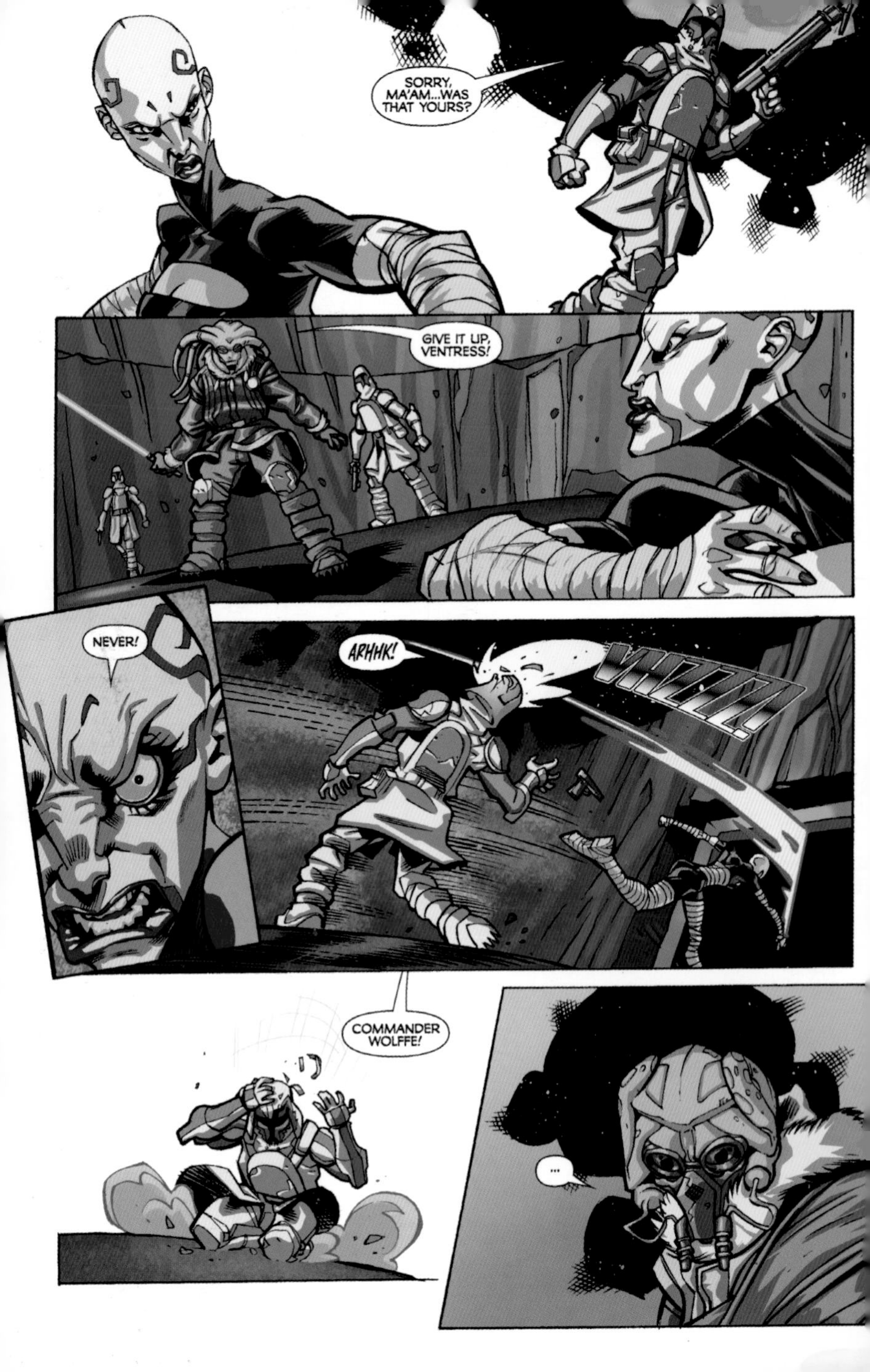

SORRY, MA'AM...WAS THAT YOURS?
GIVE IT UP, VENTRESS!
NEVER!
ARHHK!
VHZZZ!
COMMANDER WOLFFE!
...

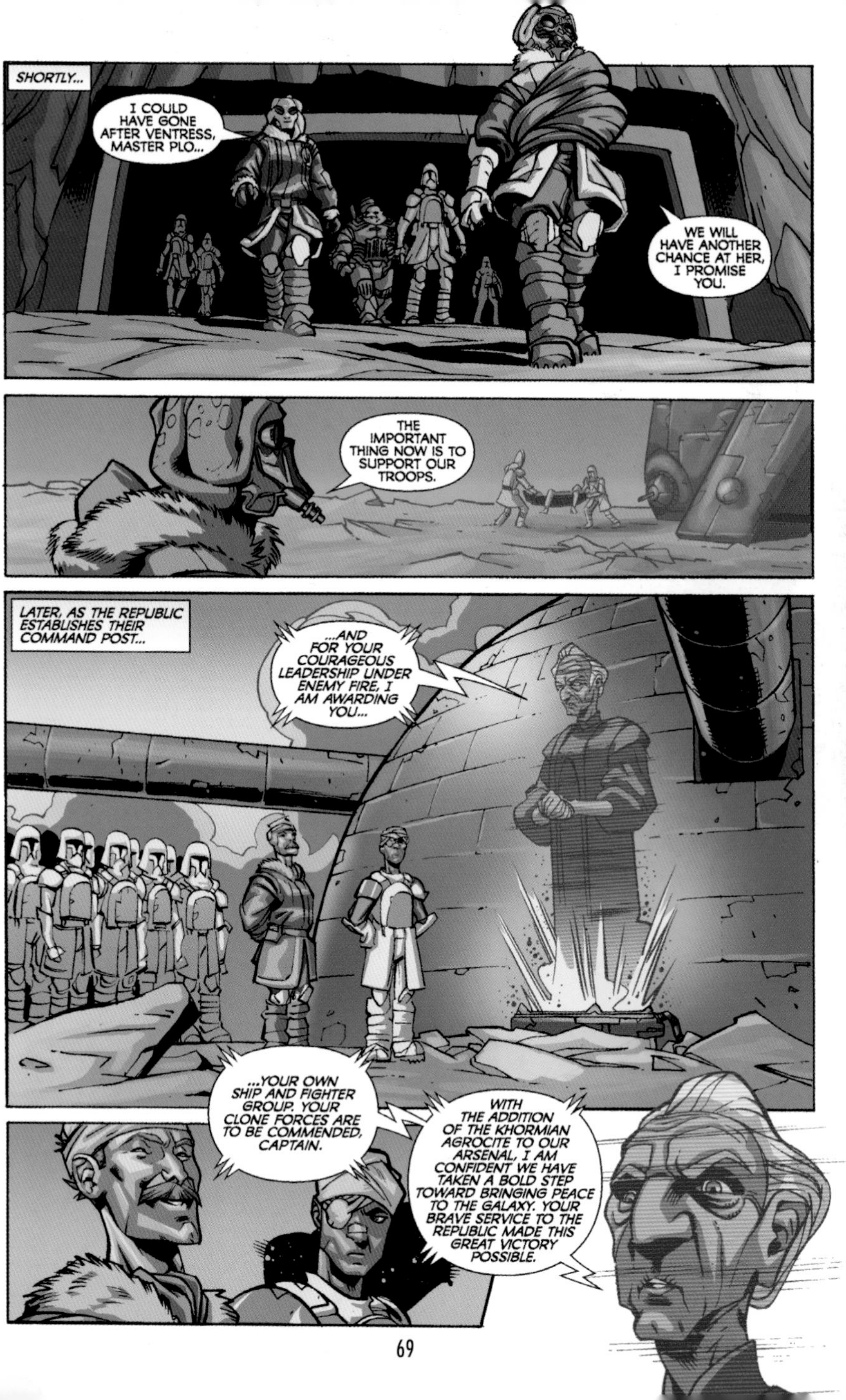
SHORTLY...
I COULD HAVE GONE AFTER VENTRESS, MASTER PLO...
WE WILL HAVE ANOTHER CHANCE AT HER, I PROMISE YOU.
THE IMPORTANT THING NOW IS TO SUPPORT OUR TROOPS.
LATER, AS THE REPUBLIC ESTABLISHES THEIR COMMAND POST...
...AND FOR YOUR COURAGEOUS LEADERSHIP UNDER ENEMY FIRE, I AM AWARDING YOU...
...YOUR OWN SHIP AND FIGHTER GROUP. YOUR CLONE FORCES ARE TO BE COMMENDED, CAPTAIN.
WITH THE ADDITION OF THE KHORMIAN AGROCITE TO OUR ARSENAL, I AM CONFIDENT WE HAVE TAKEN A BOLD STEP TOWARD BRINGING PEACE TO THE GALAXY. YOUR BRAVE SERVICE TO THE REPUBLIC MADE THIS GREAT VICTORY POSSIBLE.

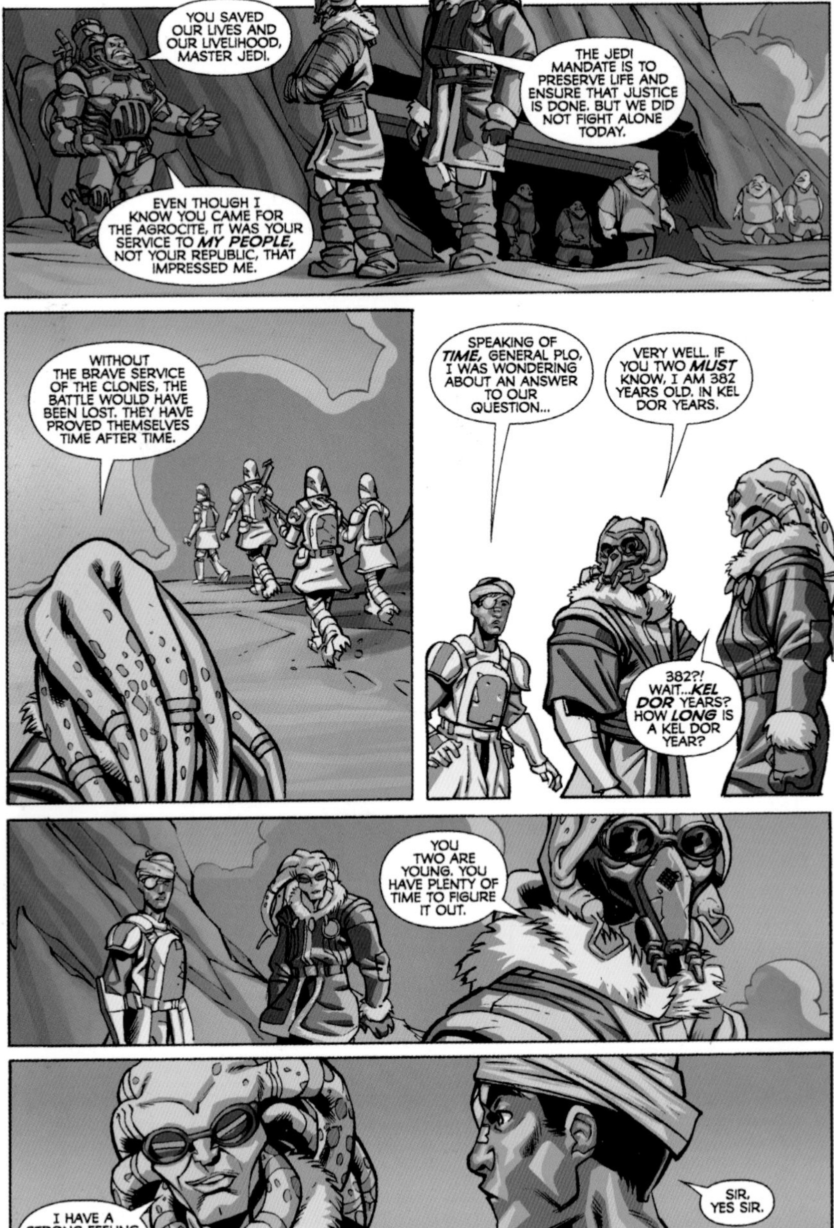
YOU SAVED OUR LIVES AND OUR LIVELIHOOD, MASTER JEDI.
EVEN THOUGH I KNOW YOU CAME FOR THE AGROCITE, IT WAS YOUR SERVICE TO *MY PEOPLE,* NOT YOUR REPUBLIC, THAT IMPRESSED ME.
THE JEDI MANDATE IS TO PRESERVE LIFE AND ENSURE THAT JUSTICE IS DONE. BUT WE DID NOT FIGHT ALONE TODAY.
WITHOUT THE BRAVE SERVICE OF THE CLONES, THE BATTLE WOULD HAVE BEEN LOST. THEY HAVE PROVED THEMSELVES TIME AFTER TIME.
SPEAKING OF *TIME,* GENERAL PLO, I WAS WONDERING ABOUT AN ANSWER TO OUR QUESTION...
VERY WELL. IF YOU TWO *MUST* KNOW, I AM 382 YEARS OLD. IN KEL DOR YEARS.
382?! WAIT...*KEL DOR* YEARS? HOW *LONG* IS A KEL DOR YEAR?
YOU TWO ARE YOUNG. YOU HAVE PLENTY OF TIME TO FIGURE IT OUT.
I HAVE A STRONG FEELING MASTER PLO IS SMILING UNDER HIS MASK.
SIR, YES SIR.
So ends the Battle of Khorm.

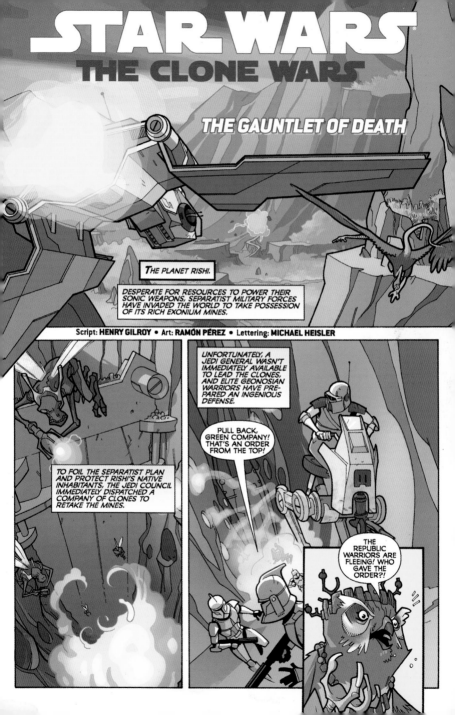

STAR WARS
THE CLONE WARS

THE GAUNTLET OF DEATH

THE PLANET RISHI.

DESPERATE FOR RESOURCES TO POWER THEIR SONIC WEAPONS, SEPARATIST MILITARY FORCES HAVE INVADED THE WORLD TO TAKE POSSESSION OF ITS RICH EXONIUM MINES.

Script: **HENRY GILROY** • Art: **RAMÓN PÉREZ** • Lettering: **MICHAEL HEISLER**

TO FOIL THE SEPARATIST PLAN AND PROTECT RISHI'S NATIVE INHABITANTS, THE JEDI COUNCIL IMMEDIATELY DISPATCHED A COMPANY OF CLONES TO RETAKE THE MINES.

UNFORTUNATELY, A JEDI GENERAL WASN'T IMMEDIATELY AVAILABLE TO LEAD THE CLONES, AND ELITE GEONOSIAN WARRIORS HAVE PREPARED AN INGENIOUS DEFENSE.

PULL BACK, GREEN COMPANY! THAT'S AN ORDER FROM THE TOP!

THE REPUBLIC WARRIORS ARE FLEEING! WHO GAVE THE ORDER?!

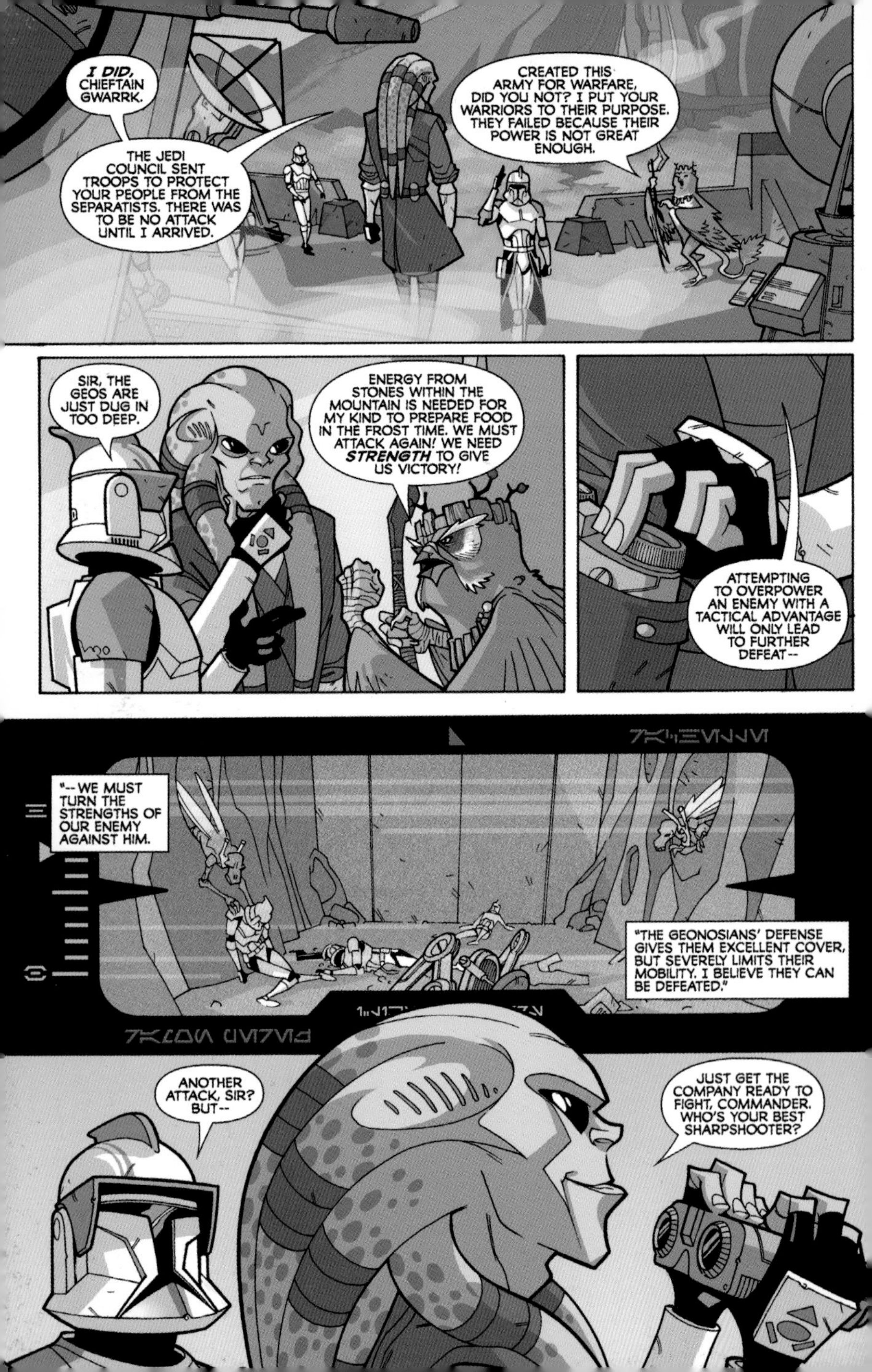

I DID, CHIEFTAIN GWARRK.
THE JEDI COUNCIL SENT TROOPS TO PROTECT YOUR PEOPLE FROM THE SEPARATISTS. THERE WAS TO BE NO ATTACK UNTIL I ARRIVED.
CREATED THIS ARMY FOR WARFARE, DID YOU NOT? I PUT YOUR WARRIORS TO THEIR PURPOSE. THEY FAILED BECAUSE THEIR POWER IS NOT GREAT ENOUGH.
SIR, THE GEOS ARE JUST DUG IN TOO DEEP.
ENERGY FROM STONES WITHIN THE MOUNTAIN IS NEEDED FOR MY KIND TO PREPARE FOOD IN THE FROST TIME. WE MUST ATTACK AGAIN! WE NEED STRENGTH TO GIVE US VICTORY!
ATTEMPTING TO OVERPOWER AN ENEMY WITH A TACTICAL ADVANTAGE WILL ONLY LEAD TO FURTHER DEFEAT--
"--WE MUST TURN THE STRENGTHS OF OUR ENEMY AGAINST HIM.
"THE GEONOSIANS' DEFENSE GIVES THEM EXCELLENT COVER, BUT SEVERELY LIMITS THEIR MOBILITY. I BELIEVE THEY CAN BE DEFEATED."
ANOTHER ATTACK, SIR? BUT--
JUST GET THE COMPANY READY TO FIGHT, COMMANDER. WHO'S YOUR BEST SHARPSHOOTER?

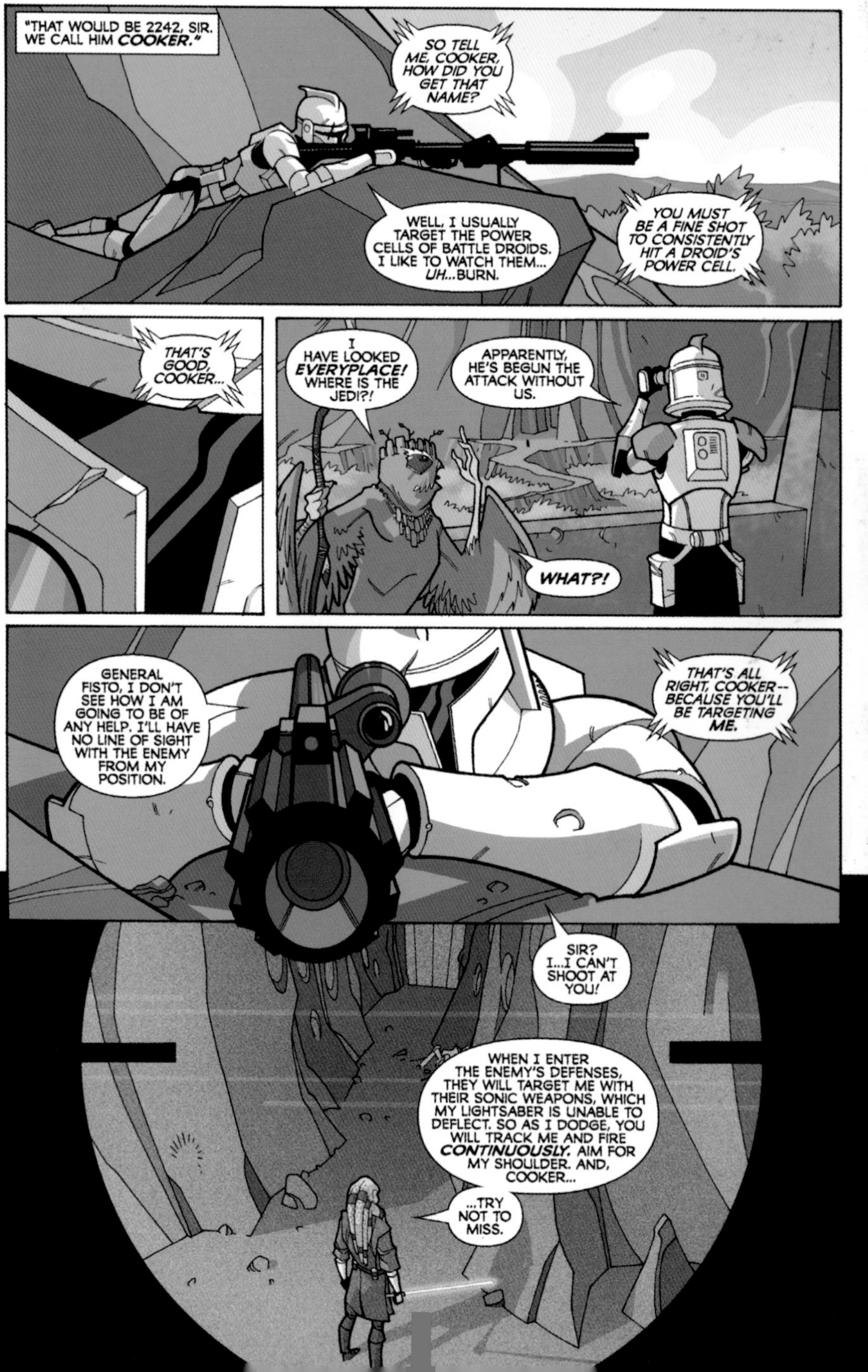
"THAT WOULD BE 2242, SIR. WE CALL HIM COOKER."
SO TELL ME, COOKER, HOW DID YOU GET THAT NAME?
WELL, I USUALLY TARGET THE POWER CELLS OF BATTLE DROIDS. I LIKE TO WATCH THEM... UH...BURN.
YOU MUST BE A FINE SHOT TO CONSISTENTLY HIT A DROID'S POWER CELL.
THAT'S GOOD, COOKER...
I HAVE LOOKED EVERYPLACE! WHERE IS THE JEDI?!
APPARENTLY, HE'S BEGUN THE ATTACK WITHOUT US.
WHAT?!
GENERAL FISTO, I DON'T SEE HOW I AM GOING TO BE OF ANY HELP. I'LL HAVE NO LINE OF SIGHT WITH THE ENEMY FROM MY POSITION.
THAT'S ALL RIGHT, COOKER-- BECAUSE YOU'LL BE TARGETING ME.
SIR? I...I CAN'T SHOOT AT YOU!
WHEN I ENTER THE ENEMY'S DEFENSES, THEY WILL TARGET ME WITH THEIR SONIC WEAPONS, WHICH MY LIGHTSABER IS UNABLE TO DEFLECT. SO AS I DODGE, YOU WILL TRACK ME AND FIRE CONTINUOUSLY. AIM FOR MY SHOULDER. AND, COOKER...
...TRY NOT TO MISS.

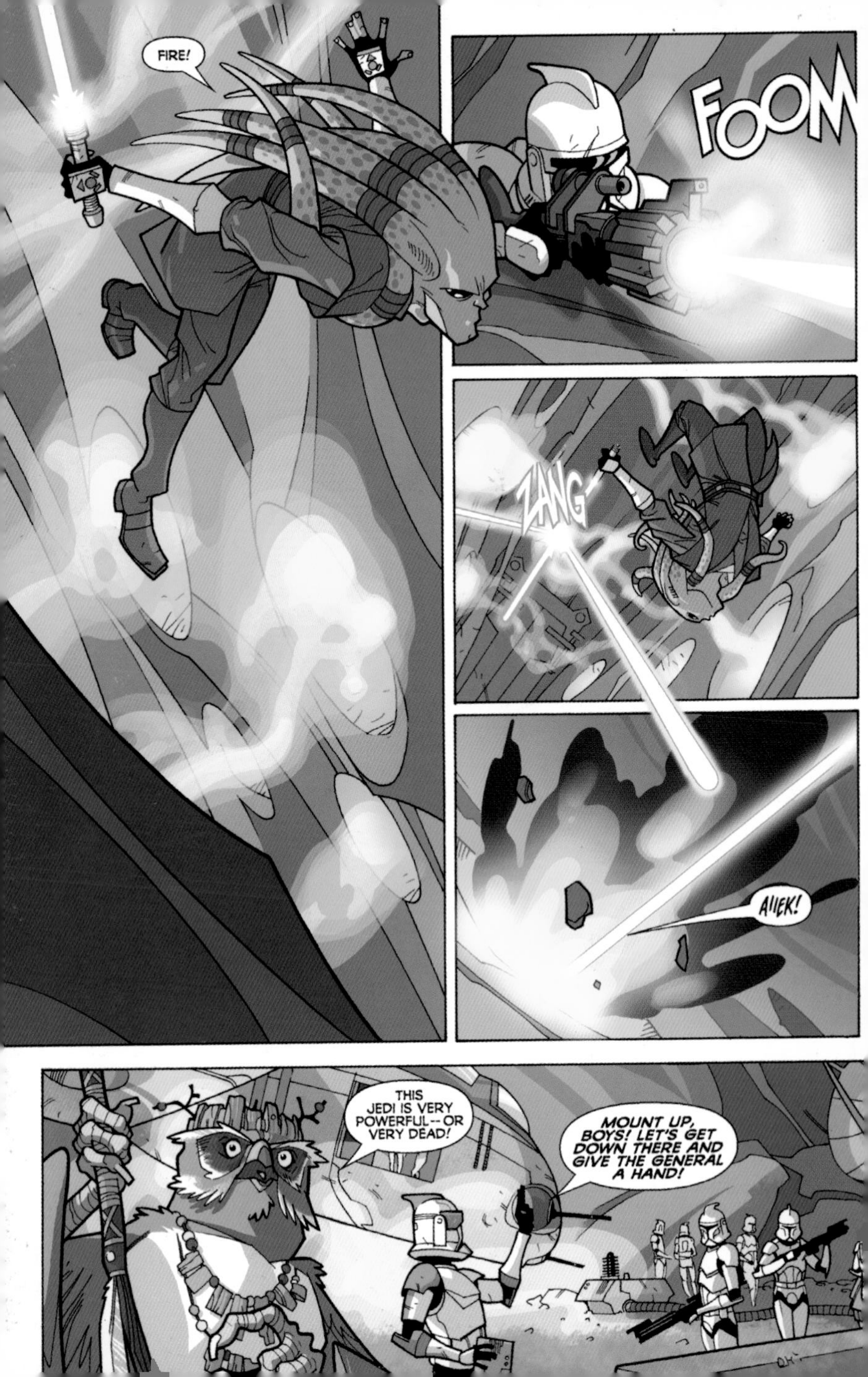

FIRE!
FOOM
ZANG
AIIEK!
THIS JEDI IS VERY POWERFUL--OR VERY DEAD!
MOUNT UP, BOYS! LET'S GET DOWN THERE AND GIVE THE GENERAL A HAND!

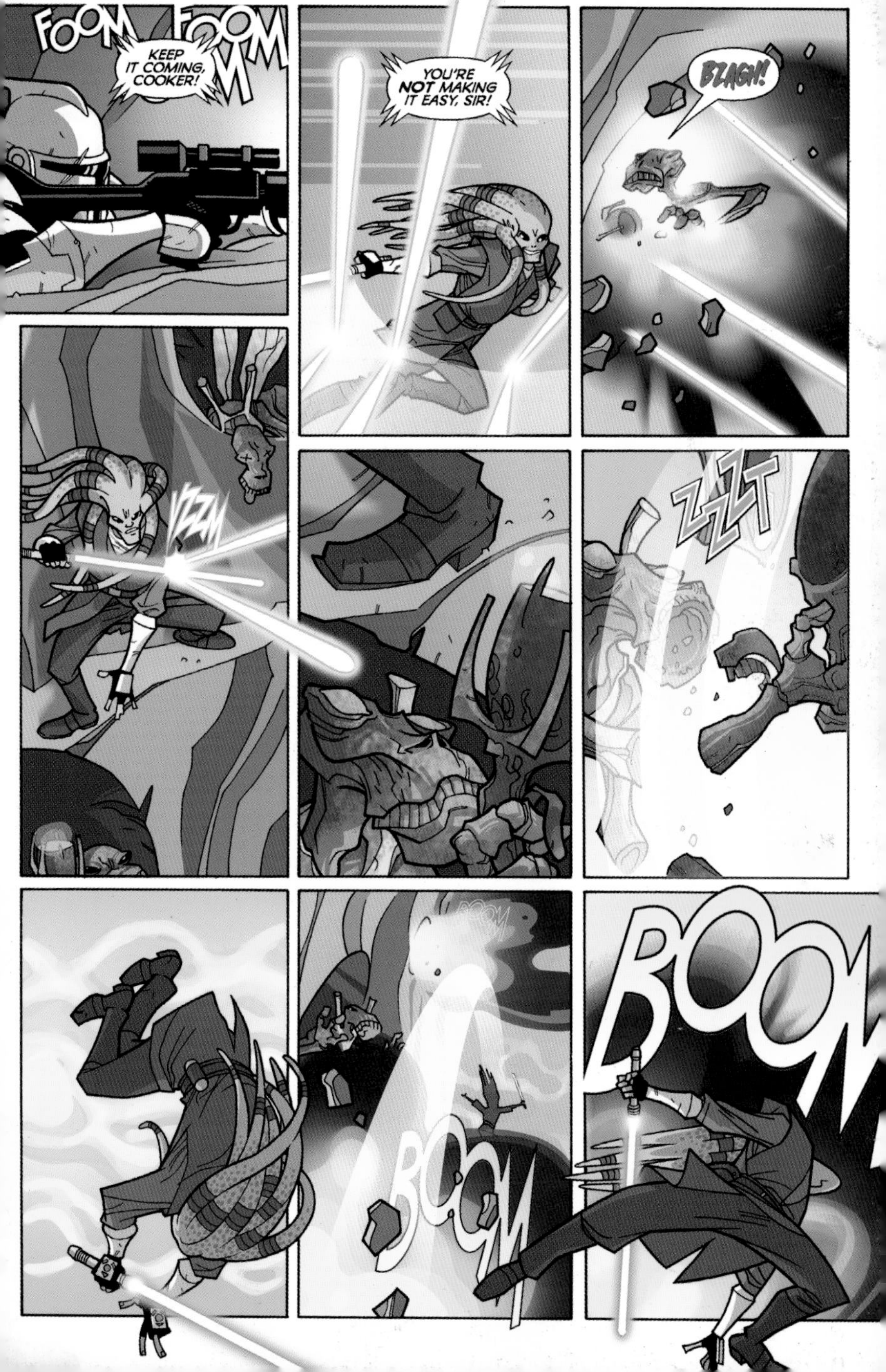
FOOM FOOM
KEEP IT COMING, COOKER!
FOOM
YOU'RE NOT MAKING IT EASY, SIR!
BZAGH!
VZZM
ZZZT
BOOM
BOOM
BOOM

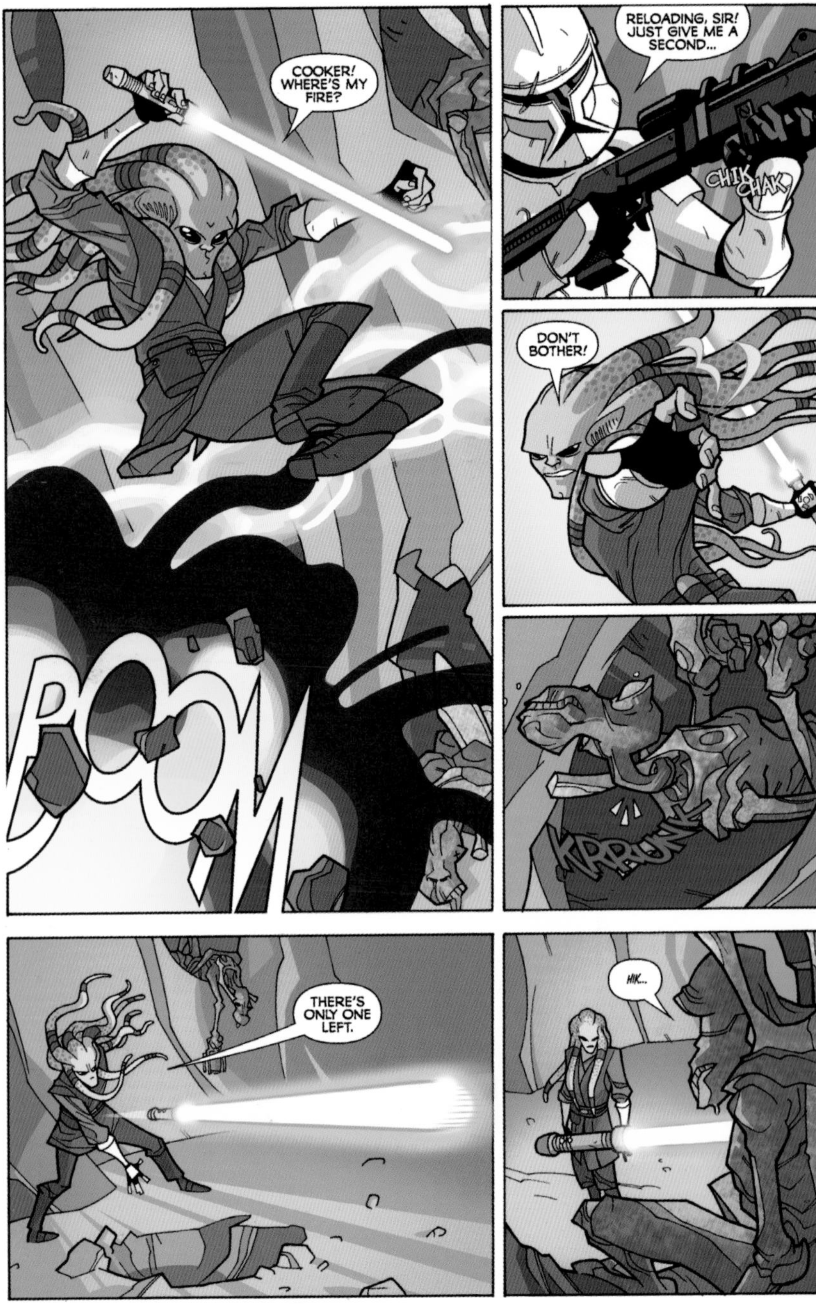
COOKER! WHERE'S MY FIRE?
BOOM
RELOADING, SIR! JUST GIVE ME A SECOND...
CHIK CHAK
DON'T BOTHER!
KRRUNK
THERE'S ONLY ONE LEFT.
HIK...

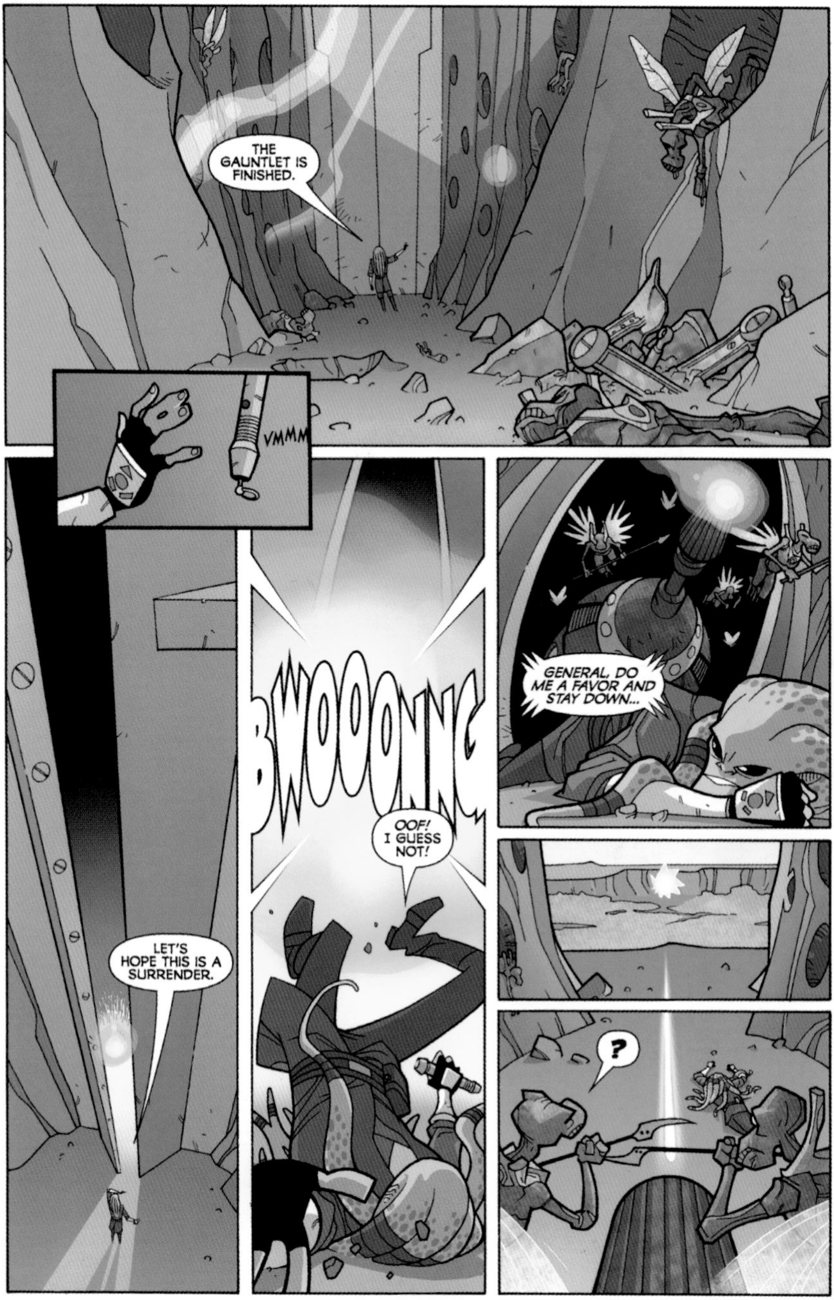
THE GAUNTLET IS FINISHED.
VMMM
LET'S HOPE THIS IS A SURRENDER.
BWOOONNG
OOF! I GUESS NOT!
GENERAL, DO ME A FAVOR AND STAY DOWN...
?

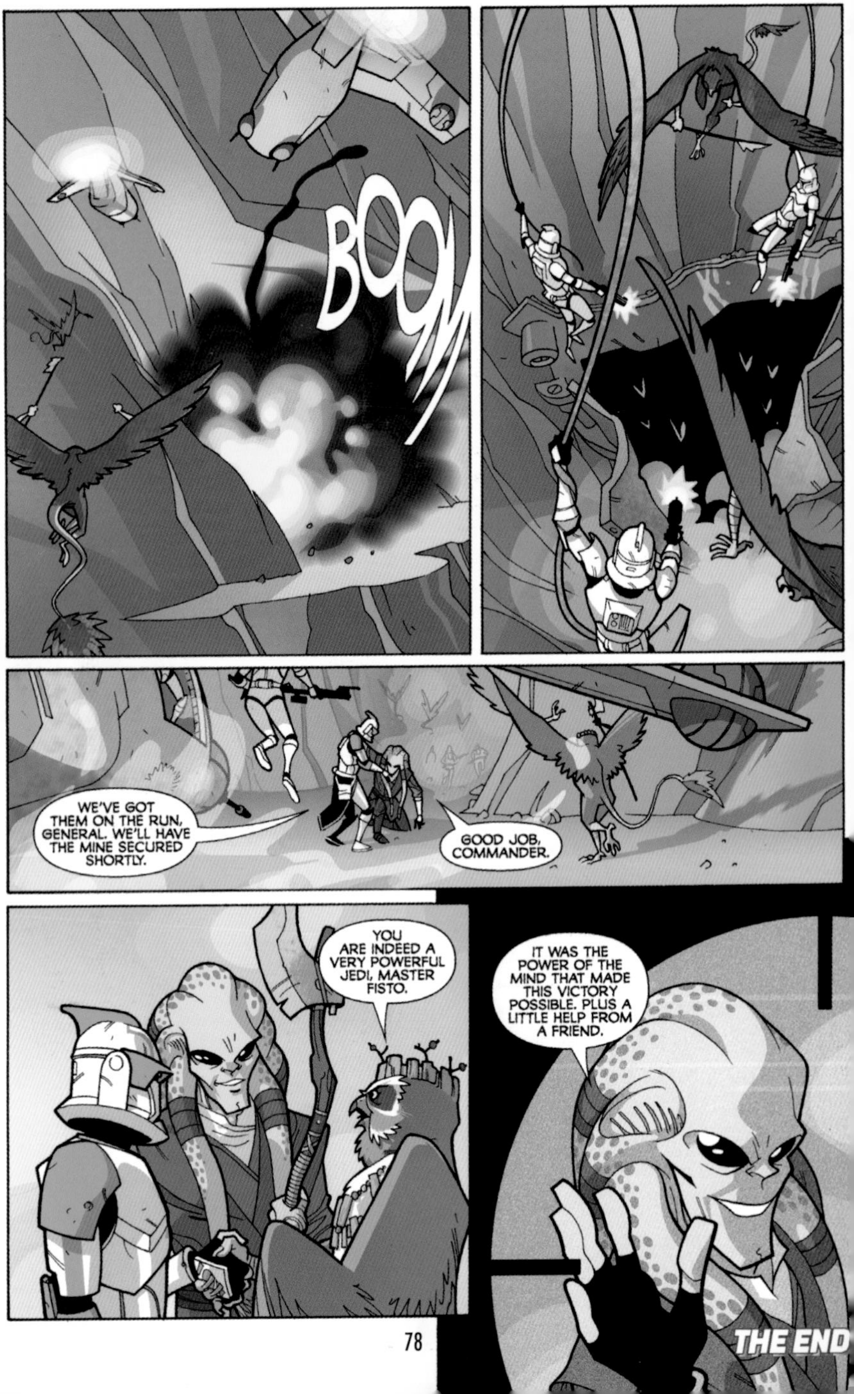
BOOM
WE'VE GOT THEM ON THE RUN, GENERAL. WE'LL HAVE THE MINE SECURED SHORTLY.
GOOD JOB, COMMANDER.
YOU ARE INDEED A VERY POWERFUL JEDI, MASTER FISTO.
IT WAS THE POWER OF THE MIND THAT MADE THIS VICTORY POSSIBLE. PLUS A LITTLE HELP FROM A FRIEND.
THE END

STAR WARS GRAPHIC NOVEL TIMELINE (IN YEARS)

Omnibus: Tales of the Jedi—5,000–3,986 BSW4
Knights of the Old Republic—3,964–3,963 BSW4
Jedi vs. Sith—1,000 BSW4
Omnibus: Rise of the Sith—33 BSW4
Episode I: The Phantom Menace—32 BSW4
Omnibus: Emissaries and Assassins—32 BSW4
Twilight—31 BSW4
Bounty Hunters—31 BSW4
The Hunt for Aurra Sing—30 BSW4
Darkness—30 BSW4
The Stark Hyperspace War—30 BSW4
Rite of Passage—28 BSW4
Jango Fett—27 BSW4
Zam Wesell—27 BSW4
Honor and Duty—24 BSW4
Episode II: Attack of the Clones—22 BSW4
Clone Wars—22–19 BSW4
Clone Wars Adventures—22–19 BSW4
General Grievous—22–19 BSW4
Episode III: Revenge of the Sith—19 BSW4
Dark Times—19 BSW4
Omnibus: Droids—5.5 BSW4
Boba Fett: Enemy of the Empire—3 BSW4
Underworld—1 BSW4
Episode IV: A New Hope—SW4
Classic Star Wars—0–3 ASW4
A Long Time Ago . . .—0–4 ASW4
Empire—0 ASW4
Rebellion—0 ASW4
Boba Fett: Man with a Mission—0 ASW4
Omnibus: Early Victories—0–3 ASW4
Jabba the Hutt: The Art of the Deal—1 ASW4
Episode V: The Empire Strikes Back—3 ASW4
Shadows of the Empire—3.5 ASW4
Episode VI: Return of the Jedi—4 ASW4
Mara Jade: By the Emperor's Hand—4 ASW4
Omnibus: X-Wing Rogue Squadron—4–5 ASW4
Heir to the Empire—9 ASW4
Dark Force Rising—9 ASW4
The Last Command—9 ASW4
Dark Empire—10 ASW4
Boba Fett: Death, Lies, and Treachery—10 ASW4
Crimson Empire—11 ASW4
Jedi Academy: Leviathan—12 ASW4
Union—19 ASW4
Chewbacca—25 ASW4
Legacy—130–137 ASW4

Old Republic Era
25,000 – 1000 years before
Star Wars: A New Hope

Rise of the Empire Era
1000 – 0 years before
Star Wars: A New Hope

Rebellion Era
0 – 5 years after
Star Wars: A New Hope

New Republic Era
5 – 25 years after
Star Wars: A New Hope

New Jedi Order Era
25+ years after
Star Wars: A New Hope

Legacy Era
130+ years after
Star Wars: A New Hope

Infinities
Does not apply to timeline

Sergio Aragonés Stomps Star Wars
Star Wars Tales
Star Wars Infinities
Tag and Bink
Star Wars Visionaries

BSW4 = before *Episode IV: A New Hope*. ASW4 = after *Episode IV: A New Hope*.

FOR MORE ADVENTURE IN A GALAXY FAR, FAR, AWAY . . .

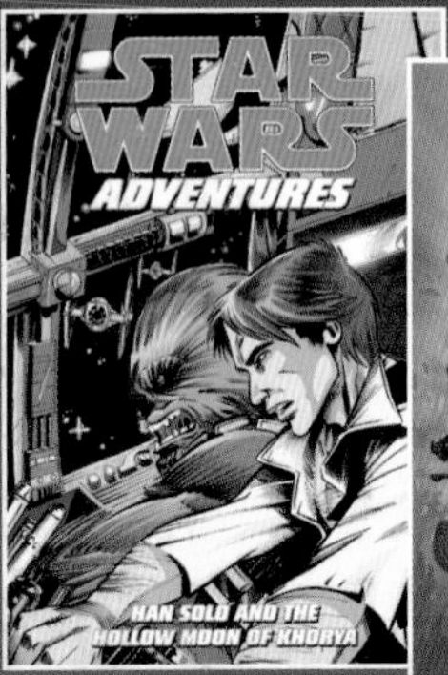
STAR WARS
ADVENTURES
HAN SOLO AND THE HOLLOW MOON OF KHORYA

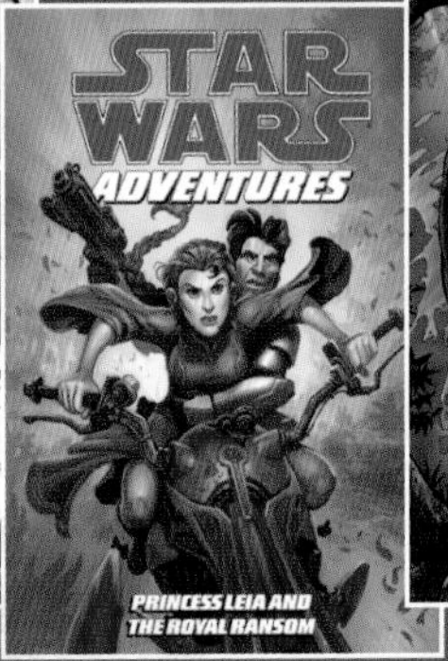
STAR WARS
ADVENTURES
PRINCESS LEIA AND THE ROYAL RANSOM

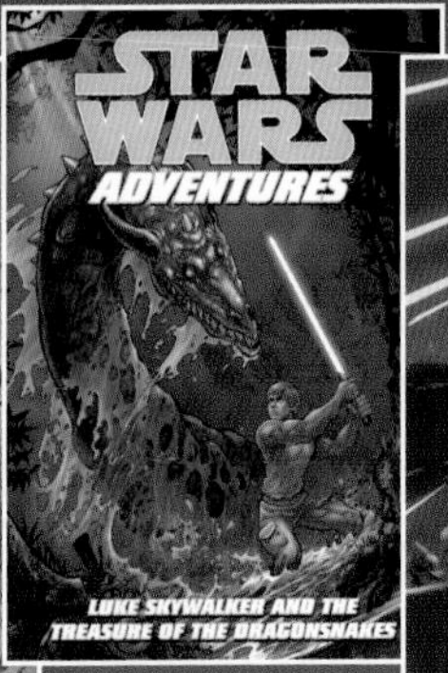
STAR WARS
ADVENTURES
LUKE SKYWALKER AND THE TREASURE OF THE DRAGONSNAKES

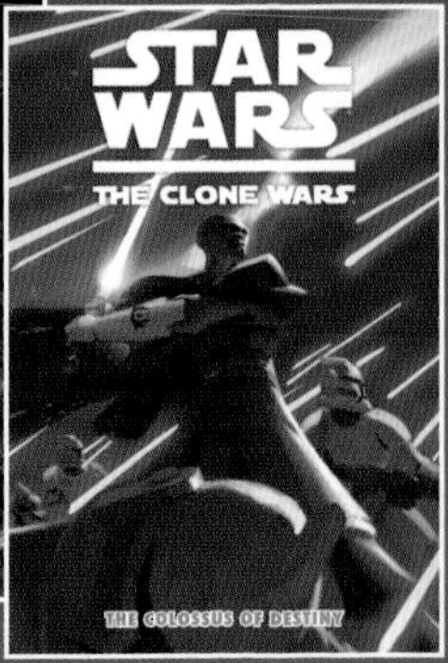
STAR WARS
THE CLONE WARS
THE COLOSSUS OF DESTINY

STAR WARS ADVENTURES: HAN SOLO AND THE HOLLOW MOON OF KHORYA
978-1-59582-198-0 | $7.99

STAR WARS ADVENTURES: PRINCESS LEIA AND THE ROYAL RANSOM
978-1-59582-147-8 | $7.99

STAR WARS ADVENTURES: LUKE SKYWALKER AND THE TREASURE OF THE DRAGONSNAKES
978-1-59582-347-2 | $7.99

STAR WARS: THE CLONE WARS— THE COLOSSUS OF DESTINY
978-1-59582-416-5 | $7.99

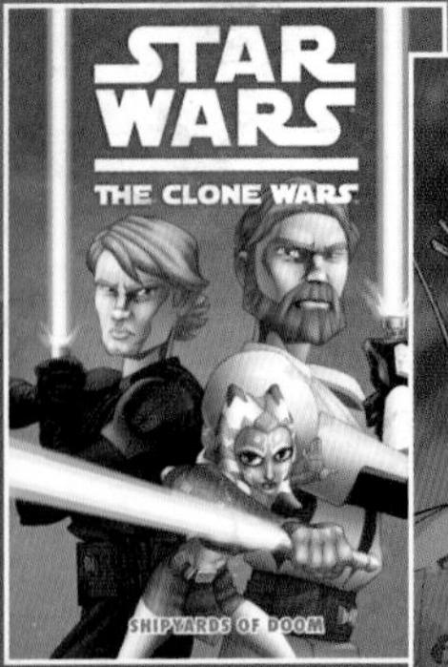
STAR WARS
THE CLONE WARS
SHIPYARDS OF DOOM

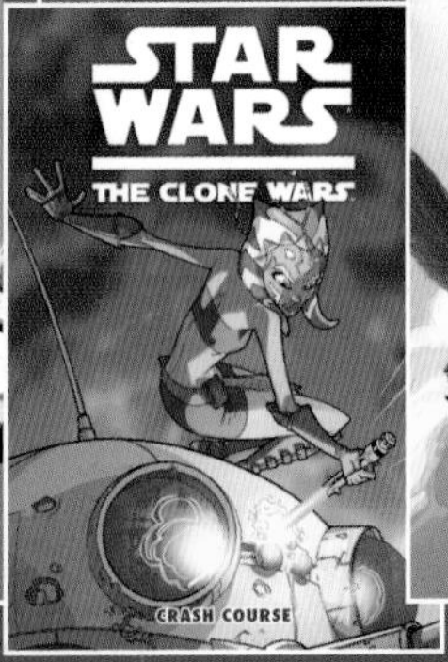
STAR WARS
THE CLONE WARS
CRASH COURSE

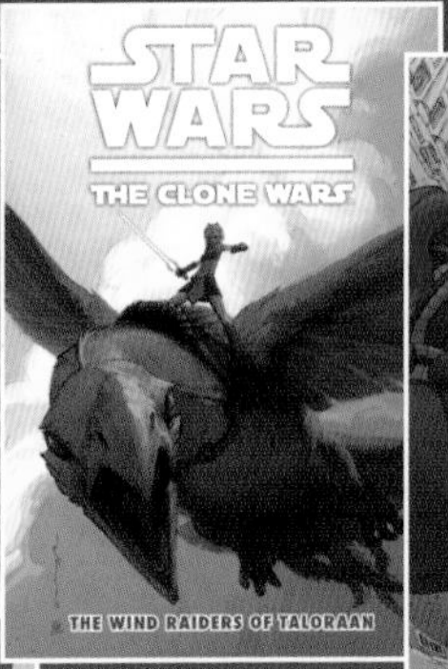
STAR WARS
THE CLONE WARS
THE WIND RAIDERS OF TALORAAN

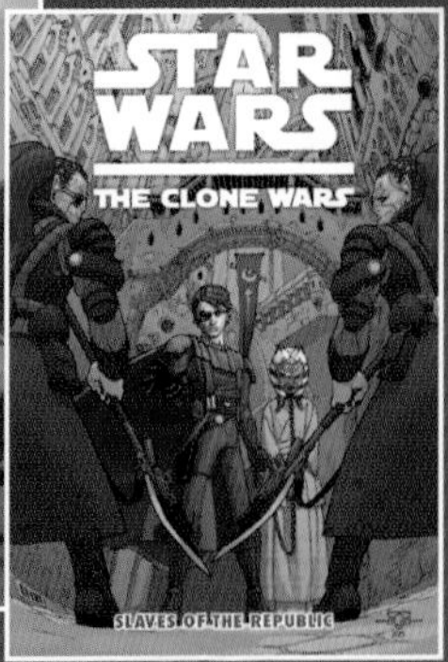
STAR WARS
THE CLONE WARS
SLAVES OF THE REPUBLIC

STAR WARS: THE CLONE WARS— SHIPYARDS OF DOOM
978-1-59582-207-9 | $7.99

STAR WARS: THE CLONE WARS—CRASH COURSE
978-1-59582-230-7 | $7.99

STAR WARS: THE CLONE WARS— THE WIND RAIDERS OF TALORAAN
978-1-59582-231-4 | $7.99

STAR WARS: THE CLONE WARS— SLAVES OF THE REPUBLIC
978-1-59582-349-6 | $9.99

DARK HORSE BOOKS
darkhorse.com

AVAILABLE AT YOUR LOCAL COMICS SHOP OR BOOKSTORE

To find a comics shop in your area, call 1-888-266-4226
For more information or to order direct: • On the web: darkhorse.com • E-mail: mailorder@darkhorse.c
• Phone: 1-800-862-0052 Mon.–Fri. 9 AM to 5 PM Pacific Time.